MASTERS
OF DECEPTION

Escher, Dalí & the Artists of Optical Illusion

Al Seckel

FOREWORD BY

Douglas R. Hofstadter, Ph.D.

Pulitzer Prize–winning author of *Gödel, Escher, Bach*

STERLING PUBLISHING CO., INC.

New York

To Bruno Ernst, aka Hans Rijk,

and Oscar Reutersvärd,

who helped and encouraged me so

much in the beginning.

Credits and permissions appear on pages 319 and 320

DESIGN DIRECTOR: Jeannine Ford
BOOK DESIGN: Richard Oriolo
COPYEDITORS: Lisa Smith and Tamias ben-Magid
EDITOR: Rodman Pilgrim Neumann

LIBRARY OF CONGRESS CATALOGING-IN-PUBLICATION DATA
Seckel, Al.
Masters of deception : Escher, Dalí & the artists of optical illusion / Al Seckel ; foreword
    by Douglas R. Hofstadter, Ph.D.
            p. cm.
            Includes index.
            ISBN 1-4027-0577-8
    1. Optical illusions in art. I. Title.
N7430.5.S414 2004
701'.15—dc22

                                                                                2004005348

10 9 8 7 6 5 4 3

Published by Sterling Publishing Co., Inc.
387 Park Avenue South, New York, NY 10016
© 2004 by Al Seckel
Distributed in Canada by Sterling Publishing
^{c}/o Canadian Manda Group, 165 Dufferin Street
Toronto, Ontario, Canada M6K 3H6
Distributed in Australia by Capricorn Link (Australia) Pty. Ltd.
P.O. Box 704, Windsor, NSW 2756, Australia
Printed in China
All rights reserved

Sterling ISBN 1-4027-0577-8

For information about custom editions, special sales, premium and
corporate purchases, please contact Sterling Special Sales
Department at 800-805-5489 or specialsales@sterlingpub.com.

CONTENTS

FOREWORD

Douglas R. Hofstadter, Ph.D.

Center for Research on Concepts and Cognition
Indiana University

IN THE 1970S, WHEN I was in graduate school in Oregon, I often used to drive back and forth between Eugene and the San Francisco Bay Area on Interstate 5, usually late at night, and I have a most vivid memory of the flashing warning signs that I would frequently encounter along sections of the highway in Oregon that were under repair. Those signs consisted of four lights at the corners of a square, and they would alternate between the two patterns shown below, at a pulse rate of about two per second.

I watched these flashing lights mesmerizedly, with the feeling that hidden in this simple-seeming pulsation there was some kind of deep perceptual ambiguity. And indeed, soon enough I realized that I could perceive such a sign in many different ways. I could see it as two lights (an upper and a lower one), each of them jumping back and forth horizontally, but out of phase with each other. I could see it as two lights (one on the left, one on the right), each of them jumping up and down vertically, but once again out of phase with each other. Or else I could see it as two lights at diagonally opposite corners of a square, each light chasing the other one round and round the square, always going clockwise. Or I could flip the direction in my mind and see two diagonally opposite lights chasing each other counterclockwise.

It was almost impossible not to read some kind of motion of physical objects into this simple pattern of blinking lights (yet in fact there was no genuine motion). And it became a game—or rather, a challenge—for me to see how easily I could "tame" the flashing sign, making it "do my bidding." "Okay, lights—go in a clockwise circle! Thank you! Enough of that—now jump vertically! All right—now jump horizontally! And now chase each other in a counterclockwise circle! Thank you very much!"

I never had the slightest idea what exactly was going on inside my brain to make me "see" these different patterns of moving objects, but I knew for sure that there was some kind of deep internal state that was being activated in each different mode, and that any one of these different internal states could take center stage and then the others would all temporarily bow out. I knew it was impossible for two of these internal states to coexist with each other at the same time. What my brain was doing when it followed "my" orders was a mystery to me (how very strange this whole tangle of "me" commanding "my brain" is, when you think about it—or rather, when I think about it—or rather, when my brain thinks about it, and only under my—that is, my brain's—command to do so, of course), and I felt intuitively sure that anyone who could peer into the microscopic recesses of the brain and resolve this perceptual mystery would surely have achieved an enormously profound insight (that is, an "in-sight") into the nature of consciousness—and thus into the nature of what being human is all about.

What this says to me is that perception is the deepest mystery. How do we convert thousands or millions of tiny signals into the illusion (and yes, it is an illusion) of seeing just one thing? Look, for example, at Ken Knowlton's image "God Does Not Play Dice with the Universe." There you will see several thousand tiny white circles against a black background. But if you move back a few feet, you will no longer see any white circles, but a human face. Not only some face, but the face of Albert Einstein. Now it has become one thing, no longer thousands of things. You will see, as clearly as can be, his white mustache, his chin, his eyebrows, his wrinkles, his aged wisdom, and his sadness. And yet, where is that mournful sadness located when you come closer, shifting your gaze to the little white circles instead? Where did that sadness go? How does it magically come back?

Or look at Knowlton's "Pentomino Magic," composed of 324 pentominos. When you are far from it, what you see without the least ambiguity is Solomon Golomb's face with its fluffy white beard.

You can easily imagine how that beard would feel to the touch—and not only do you see Golomb's eyes, but you can even see where he is looking! And yet when you come back close to the image, it all poofs into thin air. There are no eyes, there is no beard—there are just a bunch of flat gray shapes made of five squares each. Where did that ever-so-vivid fluffiness go? Where did the piercing gaze vanish to?

And on and on it goes, with Knowlton's portraits of Helen Keller, of Jacques Cousteau, of Lennart Green, of Jerry Slocum, of Will Shortz—not to mention his marvelous "Self-Portrait in Triangles." I can gaze at these images forever, marveling at their astonishing way of making something out of almost nothing. How can an array of 945 spools of thread look so uncannily like a human being— in fact, like a very particular human being, even evoking very clearly his character traits? Once again, we are being brought into intimate contact with the central enigma of human perception and human consciousness.

Each of the artists in this wonderful volume of art has found some unique manner of making your brain play tricks on you, whether you will it to or not. Try looking at Sandro Del-Prete's "Folded Chess Set" without becoming bewitched, bothered, and bewildered—it is impossible. Or try to be the bishop climbing up that central ladder, and see if you don't grow dazed, dazzled, and dizzy! Or turn the page, and find the ballerina's face echoed in the three middle fingers of the hand to her left. Do you see her eyes and mouth there? Look away and look back, and lo, they have vanished—it's just a hand. And a few pages later, what is Leonardo da Vinci painting? Or come to think of it, is there any painter there, or just a donkey with a bearded rider?

Don't let anybody from the "art world" tell you that these artists are not interested in aesthetics. That is what this book is all about. It is about finding stunning flashes of great beauty in the most unexpected of places.

One of my favorite illusions ever was a photograph taken by Matt Kahn, a professor in the Stanford Art Department. One day, walking in Florence right after a rainstorm, he saw a manhole cover filled with colorful confetti. Ever ready with his camera, Matt pointed it down, snapped the image, and a year or two later, in a slide show for a group of Stanford students one evening, he asked us, "What is this image of?" We all were convinced, and many of us said, "It's a stained-glass window in some French cathedral, isn't it?" And then he told us what it was, and we couldn't believe our brains. Our eyes told us, though, that he was certainly right. This is aesthetics, this is magic, this is what art is all about.

In this volume, Al Seckel has pulled together a magnificent collection of some of the great masters of the profound art of pulling the wool over the human perceptual system. Shigeo Fukuda's crazy objects that radically change their identity as you walk around them, István Orosz's marvelous sketch of two actors who all of a sudden metamorphose into the face of William Shakespeare, Rob

Gonsalves' eerily beautiful painting of a surrealistic multi-arched bridge that, as it curves out towards you over gently rippling waters, vanishes into the air, to be replaced by a convoy of sailing ships one behind the other—this is the purest, the most lyrical of visual poetry.

These are not cheap tricks. These are images that afford insights into perceptual and conceptual beauty, into our eternal fascination with the unfathomable, into the weird ambiguous state of seeing things that are not there, yet that are there. Images such as these have the power to carry us back into that long-gone and deeply missed period of our childhood when magic was commonplace, when the boundary between what was possible and what was impossible was totally blurry. Do not let the "art world" tell you that this type of art is shallow trickery. The "art world" is just jealous, that's all there is to it.

But the deeper minds in the art world won't mouth such silly platitudes, for they know that this art is some of the great art that is being produced in our day. Ken Knowlton's coarse-grained pointillism is pure visual magic that will last a long time, as are Oscar Reutersvärd's myriad fantasy-filled studies of twisted shapes that defy all our attempts to understand them.

I don't have room to tip my hat to each individual artist in this collection, but I admire them all enormously. Any human being with eyes that can see who found this set of visual images boring would without any doubt be infinitely boring as well as an insufferable snob. But I take it for granted that you, dear reader, are not such a tedious individual, and so I say, lucky you for having come across this book! Now go and savor all of its astonishing images; they will bring you joy for a long time to come.

—BLOOMINGTON, JUNE MMIV

INTRODUCTION

IN RESEARCHING AND PRESENTING optical illusions to wide audiences, I have found that their effect on people is very primal. It does not matter how old they are, how artistic they are, how intelligent they are, what their background or culture is; people just love optical illusions and enjoy being deceived in a delightful and surprising way. The traditional form and presentation of optical illusions, however, has not generally been artistic, but scientific, designed to demonstrate various aspects of how our visual/perceptual system can be misled. Of course, one can find examples of optical illusions in art since Roman times, but these were mainly dismissed as mistakes of perspective, errors that crept into works by careless artists. In a famous eighteenth century engraving by William Hogarth, he challenged the viewer to find all the perspective mistakes.

WILLIAM HOGARTH, "PERSPECTIVE ABSURDITIES," ENGRAVING, 1754

Of course, traditional Western art is illusionistic by nature. For example, in a painting, a three-dimensional scene is inferred from a two-dimensional image. In this case, the artist uses illusions that our brain's visual system will accept in order to depict a realistic scene. The extreme example of this form of illusionary art is called *trompe l'oeil* (French for "fool the eye"); the term refers to works of art designed to deceive the viewer, if only momentarily, into believing that the artist's fictitious representation is real. The art form of *trompe l'oeil* originated in ancient Greece and was used widely by the Romans, only to become a lost art during the Dark Ages. It was revived during the Renaissance and flourished again in the Baroque age, when it was used to enlarge and bring an element of fantasy to a room incorporating invented hallways, objects, and people.

No doubt, the high point of this art was achieved in the spectacular work of the seventeenth-century Italian artist Andrea Pozzo in the Church of Saint Ignazio in Rome. When the church was planned, it was to have an enormous dome, but the neighboring Dominican monks complained that the resulting structure would cut their library off from light. Commissioning Pozzo to create a

ANDREA POZZO'S VAULT IN THE NAVE OF THE CHURCH OF SAINT IGNAZIO, ROME, 1691–1694

painted dome and an adjacent second story on a flat surface solved the problem. Nevertheless, this clever solution was not without its problems. If you stand away from the correct viewpoint (and there were only two "correct" spots in the very large church), the illusion crumbles. Although many people at the time were amazed by the illusion, Pozzo was severely reprimanded by other architects, who criticized the painted architecture's "physical construction." In his defense Pozzo replied that a friend of his would bear "all damages and costs" should the structure ever fall down!

Closely related to *trompe l'oeil* is the art form of anamorphosis (from the Greek word meaning "transform," and coined in the seventeenth century), which involves the process of greatly distorting an image, only to have it revealed either from a single vantage point or from its reflection in a mirrored surface. A cylindrical mirror is the most common, but reflective cones and pyramids have also been used. The surprising appearance of the undistorted reflection or image is almost always met with wonder and delight.

It was Leonardo da Vinci who first experimented with anamorphic perspective; the first known example of an anamorphic drawing is of an eye, which he created in 1485. During the Renaissance, artists who experimented with the geometry of perspective made great advances and perfected the techniques of stretching and distorting images in various ways, which could be seen undistorted from one well-defined viewpoint.

In the sixteenth through nineteenth centuries, anamorphosis became extremely popular and supplied an ideal means of camouflaging dangerous political statements, heretical ideas, and even erotic pictures. It reached a high point in "The Ambassadors," a portrait of the two French ambassadors Jean de Dintevill and George de Selve, by Henry VIII's court painter Hans Holbein, the Younger. A strange shape was seen in the bottom portion of the painting, which would transform itself into an image of a skull when viewed at an oblique angle relative to the right side of the picture plane. The painting was originally hung on a staircase in Jean de Dinteville's chateau, so that the skull appeared when viewed from below left or down the stairs. Although numerous explanations have been offered about the symbolic presence of the skull, including that it is a play on the artist's name—Holbein, which means "hollow bone" in German, the reason for its inclusion is still unclear. Visit the website http://neuro.caltech.edu/~seckel/mod/ to see a movie revealing the skull in "The Ambassadors" as well as some other notable historical examples.

Anamorphic images were widely reproduced in prints, and, in a more permanent form, adorned the walls of monasteries. It was in the seventeenth century that the first reflective cone and cylinder anamorphoses were created. The technique also became popular in the Orient during the seventeenth and eighteenth centuries.

In the nineteenth century, when color printing became affordable, the technique flourished again as a popular parlor game alongside other optical tricks. In the twentieth century, the Spanish surrealist

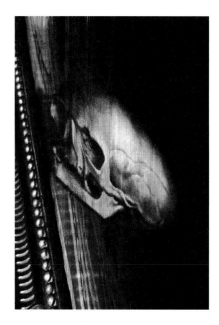

HANS HOLBEIN, THE YOUNGER,
"THE AMBASSADORS," OIL ON PANEL, 1533,
81.5 X 82.5 INCHES (206 X 209.5 CM)

When seen from the proper vantage point, "The Ambassadors" reveals a hidden skull.

Salvador Dalí (see Chapter 2) who was always fascinated by optical tricks and hidden imagery, created a series of five anamorphic images. In them, he raised the technique to a new level. Instead of merely distorting an image, Dalí created two images—the first having a completely different interpretation than the hidden one, seen only reflected in the mirror. This approach was continued in the masterful engraved anamorphic prints by Hungarian artist István Orosz (see Chapter 15).

Collections of anamorphic images were very popular as optical amusements throughout the nineteenth century. This is a typical anamorphic print produced in Germany, ca. 1800.

The use of special reflective mirrors or properly controlled viewing angles are not the only way to disguise images with a secondary meaning. In the mid sixteenth century, the Italian artist Guiseppe Arcimboldo (see Chapter 1) created a series of fanciful portraits that were comprised out of various depictions of physical objects or animals, which were symbolically related to the portrait. Arcimboldo inspired scores of imitators, and exerted an influence on the Surrealism movement in the twentieth century.

The influence of Arcimboldo can be seen also in the double-image anthropomorphic allegorical landscapes that were popular from the 1600s onwards. A typical example is "Campus Anthropomorphos" by Swiss-German artist Matthäus Merian (1659–1716).

The seventeenth century philosopher René Descartes in his *Passions of the Soul* wrote about encountering such works, "When our first encounter with some object surprises us and we find it novel, or very different from what we formerly knew or from what we supposed it ought to be, this causes us to wonder and to be astonished at it."

ANONYMOUS, "METAMORPHOSIS LANDSCAPE," OIL ON PANEL, 1600S, 14 X 17 INCHES (34 X 43 CM)

Double imagery was extremely popular during the eighteenth, nineteenth, and twentieth centuries. Many of these double images were created anonymously, and imitations were rampant as they were

MATTHÄUS MERIAN, "CAMPUS ANTHROPOMORPHOS," ENGRAVING, 1671, 6 X 9 INCHES, (15 X 23 CM)

ANONYMOUS, "L'AMOUR DE PIERROT,"
FRENCH POSTCARD, 1905

CHARLES E. GILBERT,
"ALL IS VANITY," CA. 1920

ANONYMOUS, "YOUNG WOMAN/OLD WOMAN,"
GERMAN POSTCARD, 1880

EDWUND BORING, "YOU SEE MY WIFE, AND
MOTHER-IN-LAW," ALSO KNOWN AS THE
"BORING FIGURE," 1941

distributed on puzzle cards and on popular advertisements. One of the most well-known and repeated motifs involved a couple and a hidden skull, such as "L'Amour de Pierrort," an anonymous French postcard, ca. 1905 (also adapted from earlier versions), and was later adapted again by Charles E. Gilbert (1893–1929) an American magazine illustrator, who created perhaps its most famous version "All is Vanity," which appeared ca. 1920.

There were many popular nineteenth century motifs that incorporated double images. Two of the most famous are "Young Woman/Old Woman," which was later freely adapted by the psychologist Edwund Boring into the classic "You See My Wife, and Mother-in-Law," also known as the "Boring Figure."

The Danish Gestalt psychologist Edgar Rubin freely adapted a late nineteenth century American puzzle card into the Rubin face/goblet figure-ground illusion. Both of these popular ambiguous images are ubiquitously seen in psychology textbooks.

ANONYMOUS: "HIDDEN FACES AND GOBLET," AMERICAN PUZZLE CARD, 1880

EDGAR RUBIN, "HIDDEN FACES AND GOBLET," 1915

RENÉ MAGRITTE, "HUMAN CONDITION 1,"

OIL ON CANVAS, 1934

The use of ambiguous imagery to convey ideas about perception was brought to an artistic high point in "Human Condition 1" by Belgian surrealist René Magritte. In this work, Magritte was determined to show the ambiguity that exists between a real object, one's mental image of it, and its painted representation.

In the 1960s, the term Optical Art, or Op Art, was coined to describe the work of a growing movement of abstract painters led by Victor Vasarely and Bridget Riley. Op Art is a mathematically oriented form, usually abstract, which uses repetition of simple forms and colors to create vibrating effects, moiré patterns, an exaggerated sense of depth, foreground-background confusion, and other visual phenomena. With Op Art, however, the rules that the eye applies to make sense of an image are themselves the subject of the artwork.

When most people think of an optical illusion artist, they immediately think of the Dutch graphic artist M. C. Escher (see Chapter 5). Paradoxically, many know Escher's name, but remain unfamiliar with his work. Nevertheless, his popularity throughout the world has grown enormously since his death in 1972. The 1998 exhibition "M. C. Escher: A Centennial Tribute" held at the National Gallery of Art in Washington, D.C., drew record crowds; 364,000 people visited the exhibit, more than for any other print show.

Nonetheless, Escher is summarily dismissed by art historians and critics, and seems destined for nothing more than a footnote in art history books. For example, a visit to any art museum bookstore will reveal hundreds of volumes filling the shelves with known and obscure artists of every variety but barely a volume devoted to Escher's work. This seems an affront to the millions of people—especially scientifically minded ones—who find a special affinity with the works of Escher and how he captures and presents the beauties of mathematics in ways that speak directly to them. They feel that the artistic world does not understand the "high" intellectual concepts that Escher presented, and therefore dismiss him. In fact, the art world has ignored Escher for a number of reasons. Primarily, Escher was a competent printmaker, who did not create any new techniques for the representations of images.

With only a very few exceptions, such as Albrecht Dürer, printmakers have never been able to achieve the status that painters have.

Also, it has often been said that Escher's work holds more appeal for the scientist and mathematician than for the art lover, and that the basis for his examination of the functions of art and design lay in mathematics, or even crystallography—a long way from aesthetics. Shape and form, as well as ideas, dominated his works; aesthetic considerations did not. Art critics admit that he is "clever," but feel that "being clever" is not enough. Clever ideas have not traditionally been a true goal of art; after all, there is no Great Idea conveyed by Vermeer's painting of a pretty girl in a gondola. It is how Vermeer managed to use light and color in a way that transfigured reality that made him a great artist.

REGINALD NEAL, "SQUARE OF THREE,"
ORIGINAL LITHOGRAPH, 1965

American artist Reginald Neal was typical of a group of Op Artists of the 1960s, whose work appeared to vibrate, pulsate, or flicker.

This isn't to say that artistic movements tend not to express abstract ideas (Surrealism and Expressionism do, for example), but that they have also placed an emphasis on aesthetics in a way that Escher did not. Escher was aware of this criticism, but it did not concern him; he realized that the audience for his work might not be conventional, or even particularly artistic. In his own words, "Although I am absolutely without training or knowledge, I often seem to have more in common with mathematicians than my fellow artists."

Nevertheless, Escher enthusiasts have a point, too: that the subtle mathematical beauties conveyed by Escher may well have been missed, and therefore he and his intellectual and artistic heirs deserve their own legitimate niche within the art world. And certainly for those of us who love, understand, and appreciate Escher's talents, work in this vein will always appeal to both mind and soul.

Recently, there have been a growing number of artists, illustrators, and designers who have deliberately incorporated obvious optical illusions and optical tricks into their artwork in order to evoke a feeling of surprise, delight, or even humor.

In a sense, many of the contemporary artists in this book can be considered Escher's artistic heirs, even though a good number of their works vary considerably in style, concept, mood, and presentation from anything that Escher ever created. Nevertheless, several of the artists in this book were directly inspired at some point by Escher's work and wanted to create something in that vein, though true to their own vision. This volume is the first time that these artists have been brought together in a published collection, and many of the works featured appear in print for the first time.

There are about one hundred prominent artists throughout the world who create optical illusion art, but it is beyond the scope of this book to include them all—there is simply too much material. Some difficult decisions had to be made when selecting artists to be included in this volume. Some decisions were obvious, but many were not. Firstly, we decided to present those artists whose work in a particular genre of illusion art—e.g., impossible figures, composite portraiture, anamorphoses, *trompe l'oeil*—was the most original and innovative.

Secondly, we limited our scope to those artists whose illusionary work will have "impact" on a printed page. This was an unfortunate constraint, because it forced us to exclude several truly outstanding optical illusion artists (Patrick Hughes, Ludwig Wilding, Gregory Barsimian, Bill Bell, Rufus Seder, to name a few) simply because the power of their work cannot be captured properly on a page. We suggest that you find actual physical examples of their work for further study.

Indeed, several of the works by the artists in this volume are similarly best seen in a dynamic format. To allow the reader to fully experience the delightful surprise and fabulous impact of some of these pieces, we have set up a website (http://neuro.caltech.edu/~seckel/mod/) where the reader can view the works that require motion or continually changing viewpoints. The artists who have additional works featured on this site will be indicated in the text. The website also features interviews with many of our featured artists, and therefore, it will greatly augment the experience of this book.

In our endeavors we have been encouraged and helped by all the living artists featured in this book, who have so generously given their time, materials, and support so that we could present their work in the best possible light. In addition, we would like to thank Scot Morris for all of his worthwhile comments and suggestions, Mark Setteducati, Keith Kay, Martin Gardner, Ken Rosenthal, and Doris Schattschneider for supplying some valuable source material, as well as graphic artists Alice Klarke and Andish Martensson. It has also been a tremendous pleasure to work with the editors at Sterling: Rodman Pilgrim Neumann, Peter Gordon, Lisa Smith, and Tamias ben-Magid.

We hope that this volume will stimulate interest in the works of many very creative and clever talents, and will inspire future generations of artists, illustrators, and graphic designers to create optical illusion art. It is not intended to be a lofty treatise on art, design, or even aesthetics, but as a fun and delightful book that is only intended as a joyous introduction to optical illusion art for both young and old alike.

—AL SECKEL
Koch and Shimojo Laboratories
California Institute of Technology

CHAPTER I

Giuseppe Arcimboldo

(1527–1593)

COMPOSITE PORTRAITS

SIXTEENTH-CENTURY ITALIAN ARTIST Guiseppe Arcimboldo is without doubt one of the most bizarre and distinctive painters in the history of western art. His reputation was built on a series of composite portraits made up of a variety of objects, both natural and manmade. Although extremely popular during his lifetime, giving rise to scores of modest and poor imitators, he was soon forgotten after his death, only to have interest renewed in his work toward the end of the nineteenth and early twentieth centuries. Then, he had an appreciable influence on the newly arrived artists of the Surrealist movement, such as Salvador Dalí.

Arcimboldo was born in Milan in 1527 into a highly distinguished and powerful family. His father, Biagio, was an accredited painter, and later they even did some artistic collaboration. Arcimboldo studied art with some of Leonardo da Vinci's well-known students, and made his debut as an artist at the age of twenty-two. No doubt because of high-placed family connections, he easily found work designing stained glass windows for the Milan cathedral and Gobelin tapestries for the Como cathedral. He even decorated organ cases. However, none of these works give even the slightest hints of the bizarre originality that he would later develop.

In 1562 he became a court painter for Hapsburg Emperor Ferdinand I and lived briefly in Vienna. Soon after, he resettled in Prague. In the imperial court, his job was to create court portraits, catalog the immense imperial art treasury, and plan parties and design festivals for the emperor. He was in many ways the court showman. Little did he realize that he would stay there for over twenty-five years, serving as an artist to three successions of emperors and kings. It was during this time that he began his series of bizarre composite allegorical portraits, devoting several series to the four seasons and the four elements of nature. These complex images had symbolic references to the events of the time as well as the aspirations of the Hapsburg dynasty. Each animal symbolized some human virtue. For example, the lion is the sign of the King of Bohemia, the two-headed eagle is a symbol of the Holy Roman Empire, and the ram of the Golden Fleece. He formally presented his first series of composites to Emperor Maximilian II on New Year's Day in 1569. Many of these series were rather popular, and one can see that he repeated them with slight variations in later years.

The documents of the time bear witness to the fact that both monarchs and his contemporaries were quite enthusiastic about his art. There is little doubt that he painted a large number of pictures between 1562 and 1593, but only a few of them are known to have survived. Some were apparently destroyed by fire during the siege of Prague in 1648, while others were carried home by the Swedes as war booty.

Arcimboldo died peacefully in 1593, one year after painting his masterpiece—a portrait of the Holy Roman Emperor Rudolph II, who bestowed on him the highest honors by raising him and his family to the rank of the aristocracy for his devoted services.

"SELF-PORTRAIT," BLUE PEN-AND-WASH DRAWING, CA. 1575

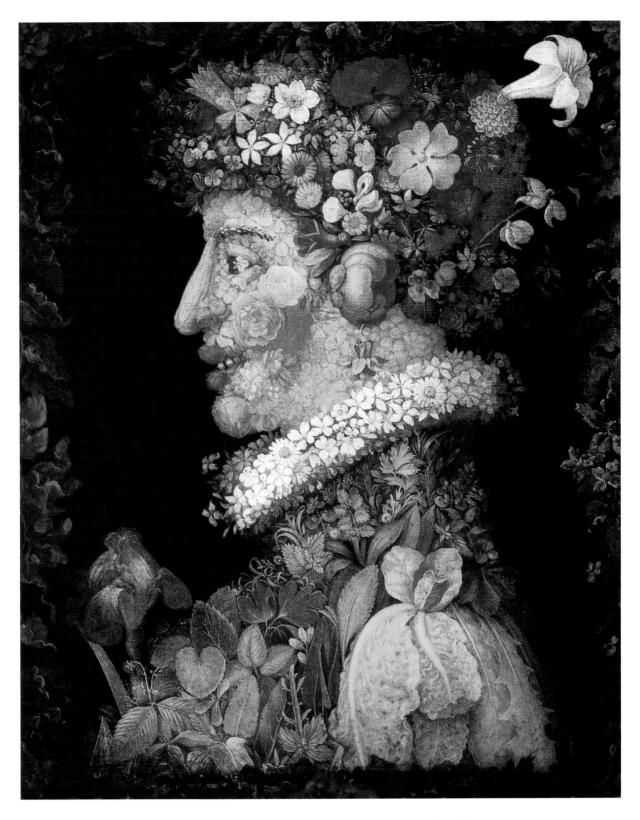

This is the first work in a series of portraits dedicated to the cycle of the four seasons. Seasonal fruits and objects symbolically represent each portrait. Each fruit has unique characteristics, significance, and destiny as an element of the Empire. Ten years earlier, Arcimboldo created another very similar set of seasonal portraits, so this must have been a popular theme in his time.

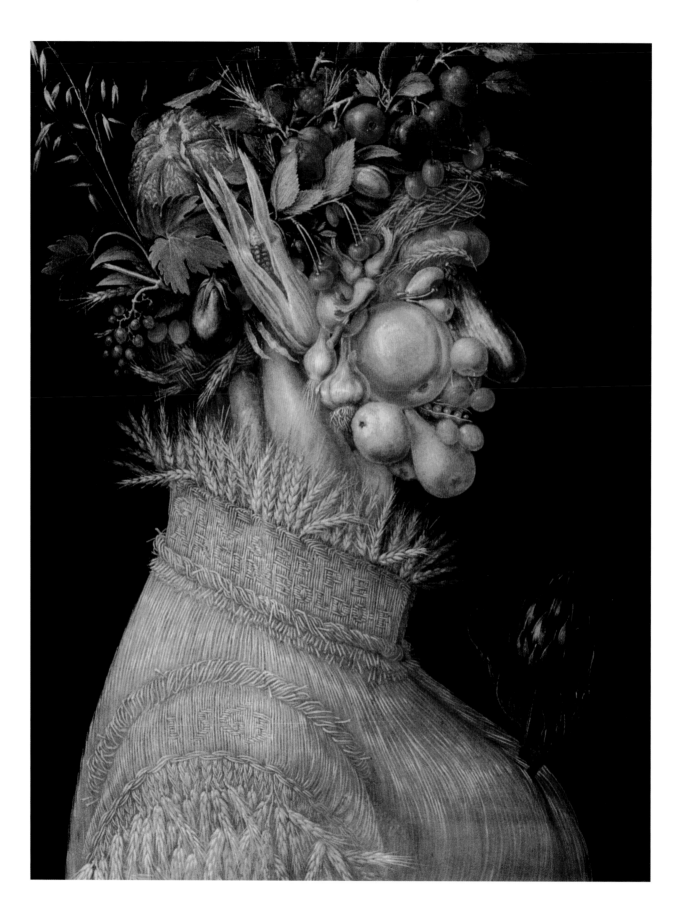

"SUMMER," OIL ON CANVAS, 1573, 30 × 25 INCHES (76 × 63.5 CM)

"Autumn," oil on canvas, 1573, 30 × 25 inches (76 × 63.5 cm)

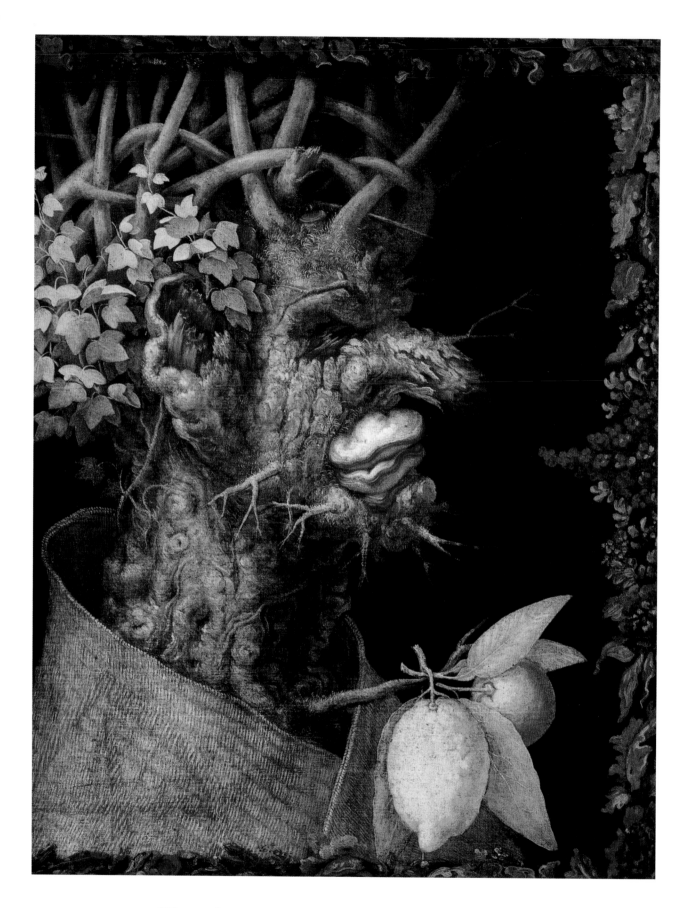

"WINTER," OIL ON CANVAS, 1573, 26 × 20 INCHES (67 × 51 CM)

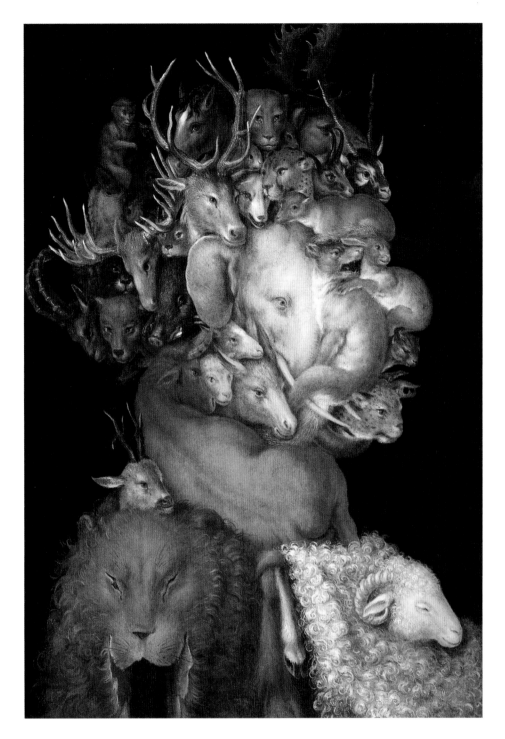

"EARTH," OIL ON WOOD, CA. 1570, 27¹/₂ × 19 INCHES (70 × 48.5 CM)

This is the first in a series of portraits devoted to the four elements of nature as defined by Aristotle (earth, air, fire, and water).

It is incredible to see the large number of animals, each symbolizing some human virtue, that Arcimboldo incorporated into his portraits. The forehead contains an Indian gazelle, a fawn, a leopard, a dog, a fallow deer, a stag, and the great beast. The ibex, an animal that lives in the Tyrolean mountains, is placed at the nape of the neck, in conjunction with the rhinoceros, the mule, the monkey, the bear, and the wild boar. Above the forehead can be seen a camel, a lion, and a horse. The horned beasts form a royal crown around the forehead. The cheek is partly formed by an elephant. Beneath the elephant, one can find an ass, which completes the jaw. The front part of this same cheek is made by a wolf with an open mouth, catching a rat. The lion is the sign of the King of Bohemia and the ram of the Golden Fleece.

"AIR," OIL ON CANVAS, 1566, 29 × 22 INCHES (74.5 × 56 CM)

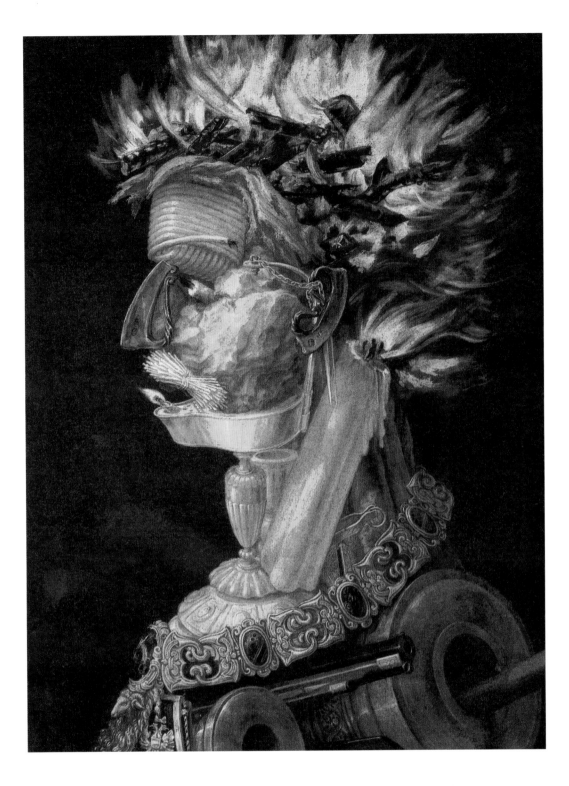

"FIRE," OIL ON WOOD, 1566, 26 × 20 INCHES (67 × 51 CM)

This complex allegorical image contains an allusion to the spread of war between the Austrians and the Turks, which, in 1566, the year in which the work was painted, had greatly intensified. Maximillian II had given orders to his powerful army to defend his imperial borders from attacks launched by Turkish troops under the leadership of Suleiman the Magnificent.

In this work, you can see fire-lighting utensils (tongs, sulpher fuses, candles, and flints). The allegorical figure also includes firearms (a pistol, a small cannon, and a mortar for gunpowder), as well as the symbols of the Holy Roman Empire (the two-headed eagle and the Golden Fleece that hangs from its neck).

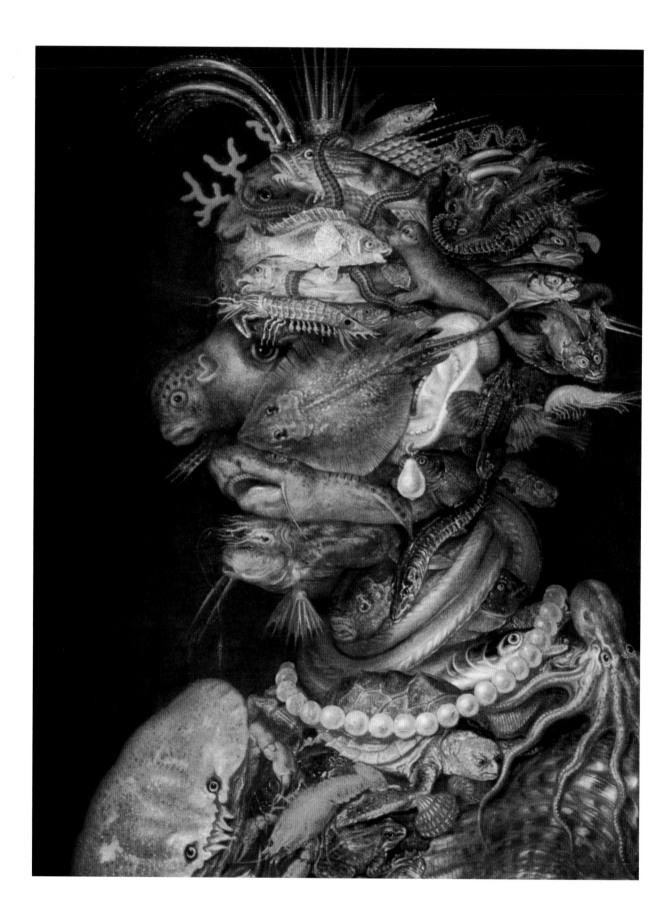

"WATER," OIL ON WOOD, 1566, 26 × 20 INCHES (67 × 51 CM)

The subject of this portrait was the imperial vice-chancellor Johann Ulrich Zasius, who was one of Maximillian II's closest advisors. A contemporary wrote, "Most ridiculous was the portrait that he did by command of the Emperor Maximillian of a certain Doctor, whose whole face was ruined by the French disease, and only a few miserable hairs were left on his chin. He imagined him as made of various grilled animals and fishes, and he succeeded so well that whoever gazed at it immediately recognized that this was the true image of the good jurist. Of the pleasure it gave the Emperor, and the laughter it provoked in the Imperial Court, there is no need for me to tell you."

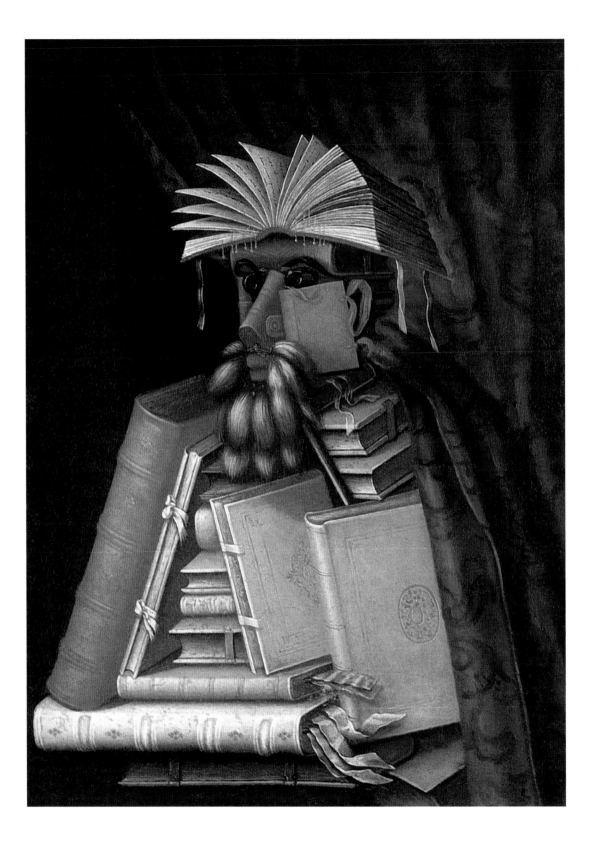

"THE LIBRARIAN," OIL ON CANVAS, 1566, 38 × 28 INCHES (97 × 71 CM)

This is Arcimboldo's caricature of the emperor's historiographer and librarian Wolfgang Lazio (1514–1565), a numismatist and noted bibliophile. Arcimboldo created the portrait of Lazio out of books, his head, nose, but an open book, as his ear. Bookends form his ears, and big heavy books comprise his torso.

"VEGETABLE GARDENER," OIL ON WOOD, CA. 1590, 13³/₄ × 9¹/₂ INCHES (35 × 24 CM)

This is the second of Arcimboldo's portraits to feature a topsy-turvy image. If you invert the bowl of turnips, you will see a vegetable gardener. Twenty years earlier, Arcimboldo made a similar topsy-turvy portrait of a cook. Topsy-turvy portraits were popular on coins of that period that made fun of the Pope, whose image when inverted would turn into the devil.

"VERTUMNUS," OIL ON WOOD, CA. 1590–1591, 28 × 22¹/₂ INCHES (71 × 57.5 CM)

This is considered by many to be Arcimboldo's masterpiece of fanciful portraiture. It is an allegorical portrait of his master and patron Rudolf II as the Roman god of metamorphoses in nature and life. Rudolf's face is made up of fruit and flowers, symbolizing the perfect balance and harmony of nature and man that his reign allegedly represented. Everyone, especially Rudolph II, appreciated this work, and Rudolph II awarded Arcimboldo one of his highest orders shortly after the portrait was completed.

Salvador Dalí

(1904–1989)

VISUAL SURPRISE

THE GREAT SPANISH SURREALIST Salvador Dalí was fascinated by optical tricks and illusions. During his illustrious and eccentric career, he experimented with hidden images wherein the meaning could be perceived in more than one way. Between 1929 and 1940, Dalí created thirty-three sketches and paintings based on hidden or ambiguous imagery. The use of such imagery and the element of surprise were central to the Surrealist movement.

Dalí stated that he got his inspiration for double imagery after a discussion with a fellow artist about Guiseppe Arcimboldo's composite portraits. Dalí at times claimed for his "paranoiac" painting a kinship of sorts with Arcimboldo's technique of creating images with double meanings. A comparison between the two types of paintings, however, reveals differences in their technique and composition. Arcimboldo's technique involves the straightforward definition of features. Dalí, on the other hand, used mainly figure/ground reversals, as popularized by the early Gestalt psychologists, who incorporated them into their theories of cognition and perception.

In addition to double imagery, Dalí was keenly interested in more complicated illusions, some of which involved unusual properties of perspective, such as *anamorphoses*. The stretched-out forms of anamorphosis—traditionally used to disguise hidden imagery such as political statements and erotic images—were well suited to Dalí's interest in evoking visual surprise and discovery. In the mid 1970s, Dalí created a series of five anamorphic images, raising the technique to an entirely new level. Instead of simply distorting or stretching out an image, Dalí manipulated the flat image so that it would have a completely different interpretation from that of the "hidden" one revealed in its reflection on a properly placed cylindrical mirror. Dalí created these images by looking into the cylinder while painting on the surface beneath. This was no easy feat, because when you look into a mirror, your hand motion is reversed: You see what you are doing right side up, but your hand must paint the picture upside down.

In the late 1970s, after disappointment with applying the recently invented process of holography, Dalí went on to experiment with nineteenth-century stereoscopic effects. He created a large number of coupled paintings that, when optically fused by the viewer, would present the scene in three dimensions. In order to see the 3-D image, the viewer needed to look through either angled mirrors or special lenses that were designed to create the effect of binocular vision or stereopsis. It was also possible to view the 3-D effect without using a special apparatus by free-viewing the images to fuse them. Once again, this optical trick fit in with Dalí's passion for creating hidden images and surprise.

It is difficult to overestimate Dalí's importance or to deny him a place as one of the most original and unusual painters of the 20th century. His masterly works, which incorporate a variety of optical tricks, stand out as some of that century's greatest examples of artistic expression and symbolism.

SALVADOR DALÍ IN 1954

"Paranoiac Visage," oil on panel, 1934–1935, 24¹/₂ × 31¹/₂ inches

(62 × 80 cm)

A picture postcard of an African village with natives seated in front of huts inspired this painting.

"THE GREAT PARANOIAC," OIL ON CANVAS, 1936, 24$\frac{1}{2}$ × 24$\frac{1}{2}$ INCHES (62 × 62 CM)

According to Dalí, "The Great Paranoiac," in which tiny figures are used to create large faces, was painted in order to symbolize the greatest paranoiacs produced by the Mediterranean region.

"The Apparition of Face and Fruit Dish on a Beach," oil on canvas, 1938,
44.5 × 56 inches (114.5 × 144 cm)

This composition combines a beach, a dog, a fruit bowl, and a distant landscape. The fruit bowl contains a hallucinatory face (which appeared in several of Dalí's works). The face is said to be that of his closest friend Frederico Garcia Lorca, a well known Spanish poet, who had been shot by the Fascists in 1936. Looking closely at this work, one can see the complex imagery where a tunnel forms the eyes of the dog, and an aqueduct forms his collar. The head is composed of discrete elements: one eye is the end of a pitcher, and the nose, mouth, and chin are formed from an arrangement that combines a fruit with the back of a seated figure.

"Disappearing Bust of Voltaire," oil on canvas, 1941, 18¹/₄ × 21³/₄ inches (46.3 × 55.4 cm)

"Disappearing Bust of Voltaire" was created toward the end of Dalí's period of fascination with ambiguous imagery. Nevertheless, this work is no doubt his most famous example of this technique. In this painting, Houdon's bust of Voltaire, the great 18th century French Enlightenment philosopher, is made up of a group of nuns, which in itself is a humorous reference to Voltaire, who had penned one of the great classics of freethought and atheism.

If you look at the painting from a distance or "de-focus" your eyes, it is easier to see the bust of Voltaire.

"Mysterious Mouth Appearing in the Back of my Nurse," gouache on paper, 1941, 17$^{1}/_{2}$ × 12 inches (44.5 x 30.5 cm)

According to Dalí, the nurse's back had a great symbolic meaning for him, and had its roots in his associations with his own childhood nurse.

Dalí's idea for "The Hallucinogenic Toreador" was inspired by a second image he perceived after looking at a picture of the Venus de Milo on a brand of pencils. He showed the picture to his wife Gala, and she showed it to others, but no one else could see the image as clearly as he could.

"THE HALLUCINOGENIC TOREADOR," OIL ON CANVAS, 1968–1970, 157 × 119 INCHES (399 × 300 CM)

In this late masterpiece, Dalí depicts the moment, when those who are about to die see their whole lives spread out before them.

The Toreador appears in a receding line of Venus de Milo statues (a recurring image in Dalí's work), from which the Toreador's head is formed, with a single tear falling from his right eye. The death of the Toreador in an arena is a standard subject in Spanish art and life. Some scholars believe that the Toreador, "who is to die, indeed is already dead," represents Dalí's elder brother, who died before Dalí was born.

The painting also alludes to works that Dalí made decades earlier. Dalí appears in the bottom right-hand corner as a young boy. The Voltaire bust, from "Slave Market," floats in front. The flies are the legendary flies of St. Narcisco said to come from his tomb whenever a foreign power invades Spain. Dalí meant to symbolize the "tourist invasion of Cabo Creus, which even the flies of St. Narcisco had been unable to stop."

The painting also shows Dalí's interest in the field of visual perception. The bottom center of the painting incorporates the famous figure/ground photograph of a hidden Dalmatian dog. Dalí's allusion to this well-known perceptual demonstration points out to the viewer that such empty, meaningless images might contain more than is usually supposed.

"Three Glorious Enigmas of Gala (second version)," oil on canvas, 1982, $39^1/_2 \times 39^1/_2$ inches (100 × 100 cm)

This is one of Dalí's last double-meaning images. The repetitious rocky forms can be interpreted as the nose, mouth, and chin of a head.

"MATHEW," COLORED LITHOGRAPH WITH CYLINDER, 1974,
34¹/₂ × 25 INCHES (88 × 64 CM)

In the image without the cylinder, you can see butterflies, a favorite
motif of Dalí's. But look at the reflection of this image in the cylinder
and you will see the butterflies transform into two warriors and a horse
and rider carrying a flag.

"HARLEQUIN," COLORED LITHOGRAPH WITH REFLECTIVE
CYLINDER, 1974, 34^1/$_2$ × 25 INCHES (88 × 64 CM)

An insect is transformed into a clown's face.

"MAN AND WOMAN," COLORED LITHOGRAPH WITH REFLECTIVE CYLINDER, 1974, 34¹/₂ × 25 INCHES (88 × 64 CM)

"Dalí's Hand Drawing Back the Golden Fleece in the Form of a Cloud to Show Gala the Dawn,
Completely Nude, Very, Very Far Away Behind the Sun," two stereoscopic panels, oil on canvas, 1977,
$23^1/_2 \times 23^1/_2$ inches (60 × 60 cm)

If you free-fuse these two images (you should look at them so that a third version of the image appears centered between the left and right views), then the middle version will appear in three dimensions.

If you free-fuse these two images (you should look at them so that a third version of the image appears centered between the left and right views), then the middle version will appear in three dimensions.

CHAPTER 3

Sandro Del-Prete

(1937–)

A CHANGE OF PERSPECTIVE

"Del-Prete, in a genius manner, materializes the well-known psychological effect, of the difference between 'looking' (usually the first glance of an observer) and 'seeing' (the second glance) when things are appreciated more thoroughly in the mind. It is this specific sensation which gives his works of art the so-called 'added value.'"

—ABRAHAM TAMIR

"A sound knowledge of the rules of perspective is absolutely necessary for illusionistic drawing: deciding either to keep to the rules or, on the other hand, to alter them and choose a false line that changes the perspective and cause, to put it simply, an 'optical illusion.'"

—SANDRO DEL-PRETE

SWISS ARTIST SANDRO DEL-PRETE is a master of the art of illustrating figures, situations, and processes that cannot exist in the real world. His works are studies in perception, and he makes us realize how much we are used to looking at things in a particular way. Del-Prete summed up his approach,

I was always absorbed with the question of how the eye makes sight possible.
Optical perceptions give us information about the shapes, sizes, movements, and

colors of objects, but they can be deceptive. I am continually asking myself the question: Is the world really as we see it? How would we see the world if we had four eyes? These thoughts occupy me throughout my work. It has been a lot of hard work to conceptualize these thoughts. It is always an external struggle with a reality of which one knows so little. It was a weary process of learning for me, casting aside the normal seeing habits. It took a lot of time and personal experience and constant reassurances from my wife, who has always helped me pursue my learning process.

Looking at Del-Prete's whimsical and surprising worlds, one is immediately reminded of the works of M. C. Escher, but it must be emphasized that Del-Prete's drawings are very different from Escher's in subject matter, style, mood, and technique. In reality, there is very little overlap between the two artists. Of course, Del-Prete has tremendous admiration for the graphic work of Escher. He wrote:

> I was certain that Escher and I were kindred spirits, for our minds seemed to operate and analyze in very similar ways. I was therefore able to understand very well what Escher must have felt when he began to deconstruct everyday phenomena, giving artistic expression to newly perceived laws and achieving astonishing effects with unusual combinations translated onto paper in ever more novel ways. There are differences between us, however: I try to create aesthetically beautiful pictures with attractive, and sometimes humorous characters. The viewer will find very little mathematical precision in my pictures, something that is always present in Escher's work.

Del-Prete was born in Bern, Switzerland, in 1937 and went to school in Fribourg, Switzerland, where he obtained a diploma in commercial subjects. However, drawing and painting were his passions, and when he turned twenty-three he spent six months in Florence, Italy, where he attended the Florence Academy of Art. When he returned to Switzerland, he became immersed in creating religious and symbolic art. Del Prete never tried to sell this artwork, but rather he started a career in the insurance industry to support his newly found family.

Nevertheless, he could not give up his passion. He continued drawing, and in the early 1960s began creating illustrations that would lead to his later "illusionary" images. During this time, he observed the eyes of a chameleon, which could move simultaneously in two directions. This started him thinking. "I asked myself what the animal really saw; what picture it had of its small world. From that began my interest in different perspectives." Del-Prete started experimenting, drawing scenes and objects that could be looked at simultaneously from two different viewpoints. From that experiment arose a new type of illusion, in which normal terms like front, back, top, bottom, right, and left could no longer be used. All the individual parts were, however, correctly drawn, yet the whole picture appeared somehow impossible. His earliest drawing from this period is "Window Gazing," which he completed in 1961. This double-perspective was incorporated many years later in his highly successful work, "The Folded Chess Set."

Del-Prete experimented with other illusory pieces in which objects broke free of their picture frames into the surrounding environment, and ambiguous images, where the meaning alternated between two different perceptions.

In 1981 Del-Prete published privately his first collection of black-and-white pencil drawings. It was successful enough for him to publish a second collection in 1987.

His passion, devotion, and hard work had started to pay off. In 1984, he had a groundbreaking exhibition of his so-called illusionary art at the Phenomena Show in Zürich. With the full support of his wife Yolanda, he started to devote all his time to the creation of illusionary images. In the same year he opened up a gallery in Bern, which proved to be highly successful. A few years later with the help of an investor, he created his own illusion themed fun house and art gallery, located in Lttigen, Switzerland.

Although a number of art critics have found fault with Del-Prete's technical craftsmanship, it must be noted that his images and "impossible" concepts are highly original. Unfortunately, several artists quickly seized on Del-Prete's illusory drawings and concepts and borrowed heavily from them without acknowledging their source. Fortunately, in the past few years, Del-Prete has finally achieved the international recognition he rightfully deserves. His place as a highly original optical illusion artist is now assured. Additional works and an interview of Del-Prete can be seen at http://neuro.caltech.edu/~seckel/mod/.

SANDRO DEL-PRETE WORKS WITH AUTHOR AL SECKEL IN TICINO, SWITZERLAND, 1994

"WINDOW GAZING," COLORED PENCIL DRAWING, 1961

This double-perspective drawing was one of Del-Prete's first attempts at an illusionary scene, and was based on the ambiguous Thiéry figure.

"Cosmic Wheels," colored pencil drawing, 1961

"THE GATEWAY TO THE FOURTH DIMENSION," COLORED PENCIL DRAWING, 1966

This is Del-Prete's attempt to represent the illusion of a fourth dimension by neutralizing the directional perceptions of "front" and "back." Thus, the viewer has the impression that all the corners are at the back, although logically this cannot be the case.

"THE GARDEN FENCE," COLORED PENCIL DRAWING, 1969

Cover either end of the fence to see the paradox. The boards are aligned both horizontally and vertically. The drawing is based on an impossible triangle.

"NOMAD," COLORED PENCIL DRAWING, 1973

This is one of Del-Prete's first attempts at transforming an ambiguous image. Although in this picture the same fragment is visible no less than three times, it undergoes a complete change owing to several major additions. At the top, a bullock is resting under a shrub. In the middle, a nomad offers a water bag to the bullock. And at the bottom, one can see the expressive face of a scholar: the difference is made by adding the lines for the top of his head and forehead.

"ROMEO AND JULIET," COLORED PENCIL DRAWING, 1974

According to Del-Prete, this scene represents "a realistic image of the ancient theme of impossible love." The two hands also meet in an impossible way: they are joined in the corner, which is facing in, yet their fingers appear to be facing away from the corner.

"THE FESTIVAL OF BACCHUS," COLORED PENCIL DRAWING, 1974

This image contains a remarkable transformation that moves from the bottom of the illustration to the top. At the bottom you can see two small figures: On the left is a man holding a wine glass, and on the right a woman is carrying a tray with wine glasses. There is a festive atmosphere as Bacchus makes his appearance. In his hands he holds the two elated figures. He slowly brings them together so that they can toast each other's health. The transformation of the festival is complete. If you examine the inebriated face of Bacchus, you will see that it contains the two celebrants.

Das gekrümmte Schachbrett

Sandro Del-Prete

"THE FOLDED CHESS SET," COLORED PENCIL DRAWING, 1975

This is perhaps Del-Prete's most popular work, and subsequent artists have heavily borrowed from it. It incorporates the same double-perspective, in both the chess board and the ladders, that he used earlier in "Window Gazing."

"GESTURE OF A DANCER," COLORED PENCIL DRAWING, 1978

On the left is the gesture of the hand of the dancer, who holds the image of the dancer on the right. In the palm of the left hand one can just perceive the dancer's face and chest. The left hand is transformed into the dancer on the right by slightly by altering the middle fingers.

"THE CRUSADER OF THE LATTICE FENCE," COLORED PENCIL DRAWING, 1978

"Incident on a Railway Bridge," colored pencil drawing, 1981

This is another example of Del-Prete's use of impossible double-perspective. Will the trains collide? It also incorporates the artist's whimsical use of a scene breaking out of its own picture frame—which is also a picture.

"Saint George and the Dragon," colored pencil drawing, 1986

This image incorporates a figure/ground perceptual reversal. Can you find both a portrait of St. George and a depiction of him slaying the dragon? Look at Saint George's hair to see the battle scene.

"THE MESSAGE OF DOLPHINS," COLORED PENCIL DRAWING, 1987

This image incorporates a figure/ground perceptual reversal, and is an excellent example of one's viewpoint being primed by experience. If you are young and innocent, and have not been "ruined" yet, you will likely perceive a group of—yes—dolphins. Adults, on the other hand, will probably see a couple in a suggestive embrace. If you are having trouble perceiving the dolphins, just reverse figure and ground: What normally constitutes the ground (dark areas), becomes a group of small dolphins (the figures).

At a public exhibition that the author held at the University of Cambridge, it was tremendous fun to watch the adults and the very young children argue about the meaning of this image. Adults would exclaim to their children, "What dolphins?" This image was also displayed in an illusion exhibit gallery at the Museum of Science in Boston. When asked if there was any controversy about displaying this image, the curators replied that once a group of nuns had objected, but were quickly silenced when told that one's perception is based upon past experience.

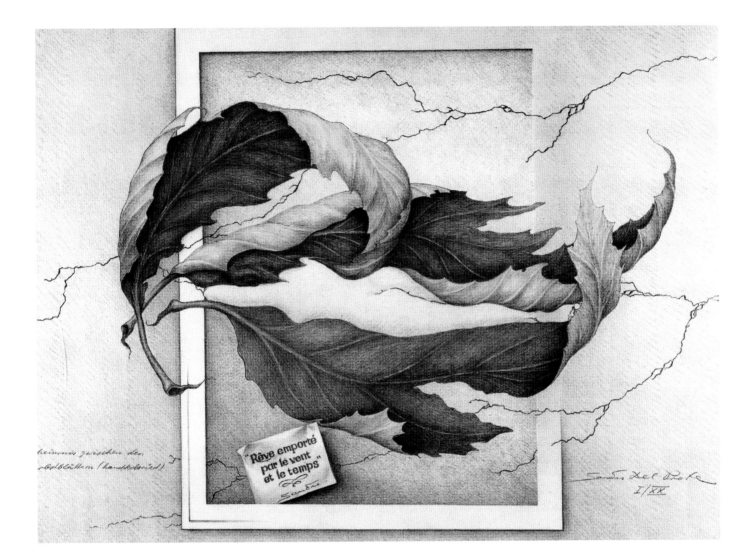

Rêve emporté
par le vent
et le temps

"**Secret Between Fall Leaves**," colored pencil drawing, 1991

A nude woman is found hidden in the leaves.

Leonardo da Vinci   *Sandro Del-Prete*

"Homage to Leonardo da Vinci," colored pencil drawing, 1992

This ambiguous scene is based on Leonardo da Vinci's trip through the Alps on a mule in 1516. It was on this journey that da Vinci carried with him some valuable paintings, such as the "Mona Lisa," which he intended to give to the King of France. Here, Del-Prete depicts da Vinci's ride, while at the same time da Vinci contemplates working on a painting. The double image, seen in both the profile and the drawing on the right, can be seen as either da Vinci's self-portrait or his ride on a mule through the Alps.

"THE FLOWERING OF LOVE," COLORED PENCIL DRAWING, 1994

Can you see the couple hiding in the rose petals?

CHAPTER 4

Jos De Mey

(1928–)

PARADOXICAL WORLDS

"Art that only satisfies the mind is interesting. Art that only satisfies the eye is superficial. That's why I always look for art that is both interesting and aesthetically satisfying."

—JOS DE MEY

BELGIAN ARTIST JOS DE MEY is a master of creating impossible worlds that can exist only on his canvas. His worlds are simultaneously realistic and unrealistic; therein lies their great paradox.

De Mey is proud of his Flemish heritage, and enjoys creating scenes that evoke a typically Flemish environment. He populates these scenes with figures derived from the works of Pieter Bruegel, René Magritte, and M. C. Escher. The elements of architecture, scenery, figuration, and application of color have strong Flemish roots, in contrast with Escher, whose classic works were for the most part completely devoid of color, and who used primarily Italian architecture and scenery in his images.

Many of De Mey's images portray an owl, a symbolic representation of the artist's alterego. According to De Mey, "The owl, in the Dutch language, is the symbol of theoretical knowledge and at the same time the image of the fool or one who pretends being stupid."

Jos De Mey was born in 1928 in the Belgian village of Sint-Denijs-Westrem. He studied at the Academy of Fine Arts in Ghent, and at the age of twenty-two was appointed lecturer in interior design and color in that same academy. His early work was in furniture design and architecture. In 1956 he attended an exhibition of the works of Escher, which had an enormous impact on him. Escher had not yet branched out into prints with impossible figures, and most of his work at that time involved tessellations or tiling the visual plane. In 1959 one of De Mey's colleagues gave him the classic paper on impossible figures authored by the father-and-son team of Lionel and Roger Penrose (the same article had influenced Escher). Thus, De Mey's interest was similarly piqued to create impossible figures, even though his career at that time still involved designing furniture.

It was not until about 1968 that De Mey decided to leave his successful career of interior architecture and design for the more risky profession of professional artist. In this regard, he wanted to depict things that could only exist as a "painting," and therefore he started to create colorful abstract illusory figures based mainly on those of Armand Thiéry and Joseph Albers. De Mey's early work generally showed objects hanging in a nonexistent space, as seen in his 1979 work "Beautiful Building for a Big Belgian City." They were representations that had neither a bottom or top side, or left or right side, for that matter.

In the same period he started experimenting with impossible figures; in 1976, his works became much more figurative, and he started incorporating them into scenes. He wanted to incorporate

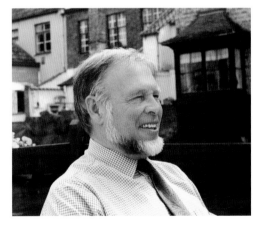

trompe l'oeil effects, with particular attention paid to light and shadow. This was a twofold challenge for him, because his preliminary training and his teaching profession had always focused on design and not on figurative images. He had to acquire new talents in order to be able to create a realistic environment for his impossible architecture. Furthermore, in his design work, he had worked for years in a disciplined fashion to avoid ambiguities, which he now wanted to promote. By creating impossible yet realistic scenes, De Mey was able to distinguish himself from the anonymous international abstractness in painting that was prevalent. "I could experience the pleasure of being able to represent something that couldn't be and do it in such a convincing way that one is likely to think that it really could exist…If you want to draw attention to something impossible you must try to deceive first yourself and then your audience, by presenting your work in such a way that the impossible element is veiled and a superficial observer would not even notice it."

De Mey's works normally feature long titles that not only give a description of the works, but that very often make them seem even more mysterious. Unfortunately, most of the titles lose their meaning in translation, because they are puns that can be best understood in their native tongue.

"Beautiful Building for a Big Belgian City," acrylic on canvas, 1979,
43¹/₄ × 37¹/₂ inches (110 × 95 cm)

"Strange Panopticon Construction for Parrots and Family," acrylic on canvas, 1987,
$39^1/_2 \times 33^1/_2$ inches (100×85.5 cm)

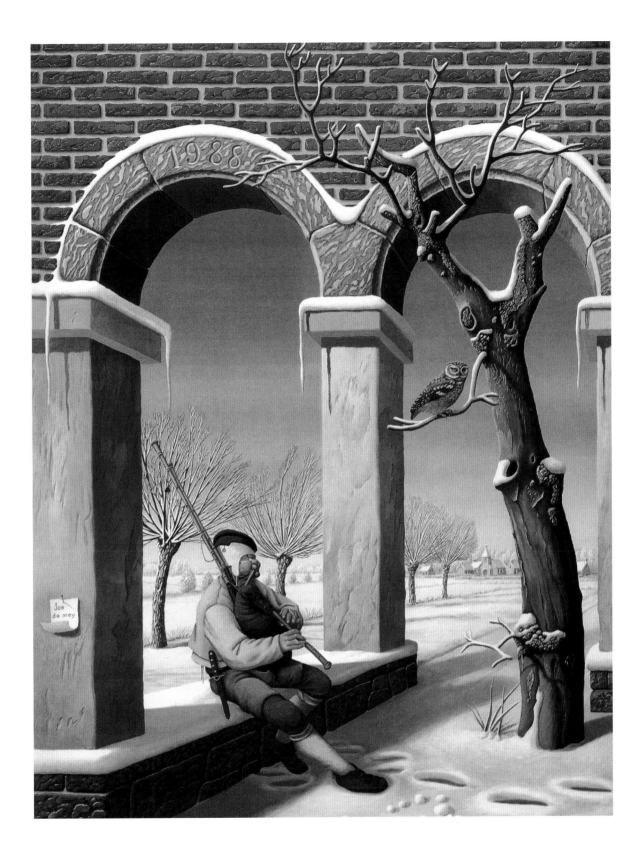

"Melancholy Tunes on a Flemish Winter's Day," acrylic on canvas, 1988,
35 1/2 × 27 1/2 inches (90 × 70 cm)

How does that left column come forward?

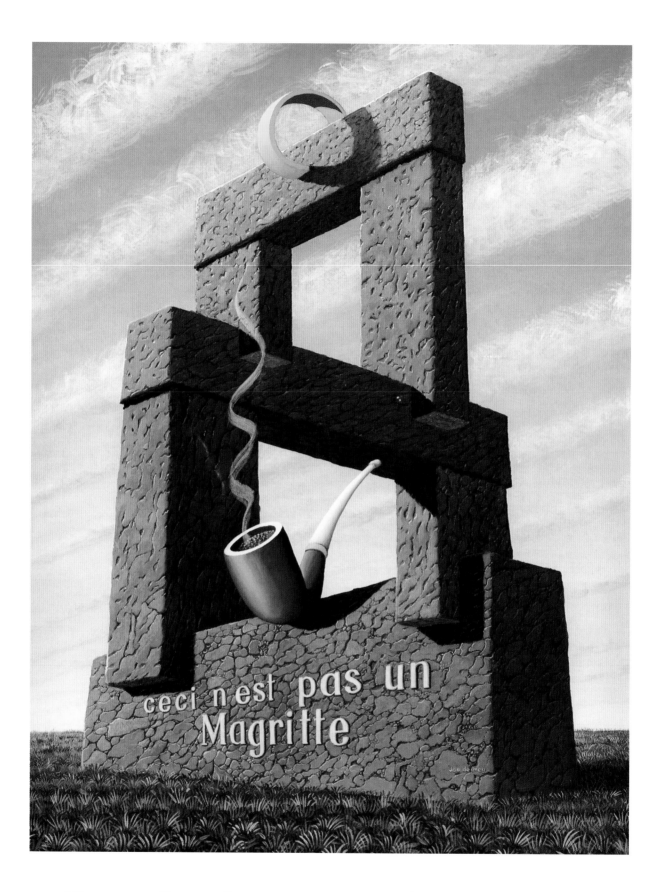

"THIS IS NOT A MAGRITTE," ACRYLIC ON CANVAS, 1989, $23^1/_2 \times 19^1/_2$ INCHES (60×50 CM)

A visual pun on René Magritte's famous play on imagery, "this is not a pipe" (*ceçi n'est pas une pipe*).

"Party for Bruegel in a Snowy Landscape in Winter," acrylic on canvas, 1989,
27^1/$_2$ × 35^1/$_2$ inches (70 × 90 cm)

"Portrait of an Invisible Man," acrylic on canvas, 1989, $19^{1}/_{2} \times 15^{1}/_{2}$ inches (50×40 cm)

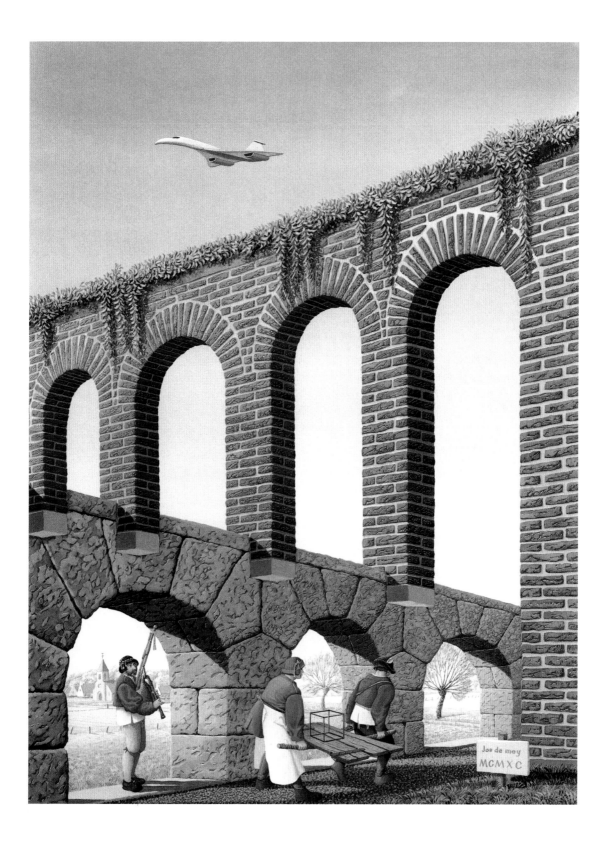

"Two Individuals Take the Long Way Around an Aqueduct," acrylic on canvas, 1990,
$31^1/_2 \times 23^1/_2$ inches (80 × 60 cm)

The bottom of the aqueduct is perpendicular to the top. This is similar to the construction seen in Escher's first impossible print, "Belvedere" (1961).

"A Window with an Outside and Inside View," acrylic on canvas, 1994,
23 1/2 × 19 1/2 inches (60 × 50 cm)

The figure contemplating the impossible cube is based on the one found in M. C. Escher's graphic print of an impossible building, "Belvedere." The Penrose impossible triangle, which has a two-dimensional appearance on the sheet of paper, takes on a three-dimensional appearance when incorporated into the windowsill.

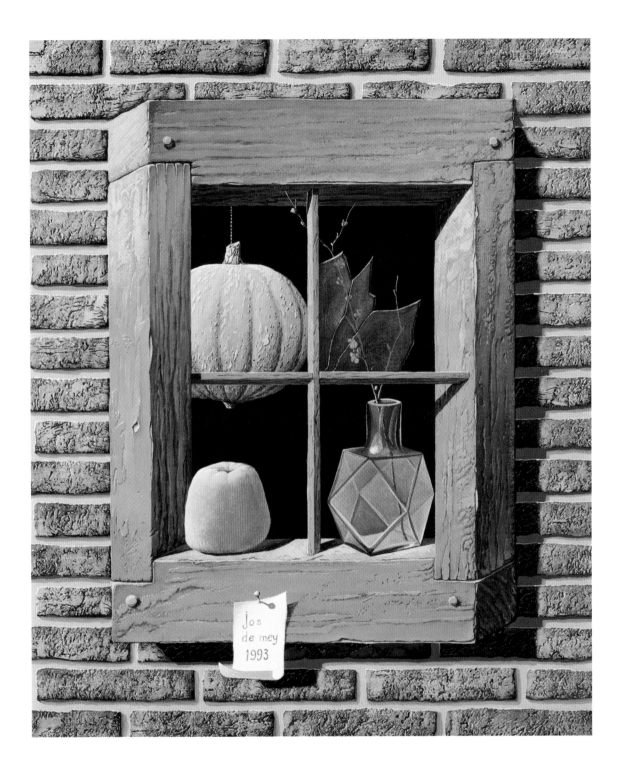

"STILL-LIFE IN TWO WAY WINDOW," ACRYLIC ON CANVAS, 1993, 23^1/$_2$ × 19^1/$_2$ INCHES (60 × 50 CM)

The window frame twists in an impossible way.

"Reconstruction of a Strange Monolith," acrylic on canvas, 1995,
$27^1/_2 \times 35^1/_2$ inches (70×90 cm)

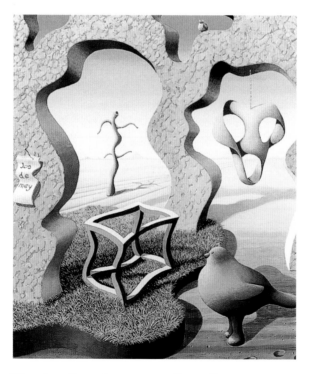

"Botéro-Bird Admiring a Soft Construction
of Jos De Mey," acrylic on canvas, 1996

"The Painter's Waiting Room," acrylic on canvas, 1996, $31^{1}/_{2} \times 23^{1}/_{2}$ inches (80 × 60 cm)

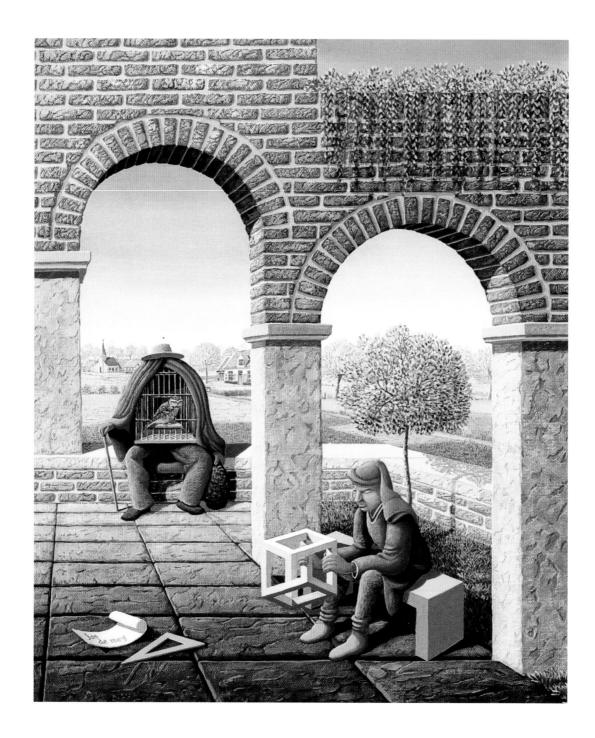

"Escher's Thinker Observed by Magritte's Therapist," acrylic on canvas, 1997

M. C. Escher

(1898–1972)

MASTER OF MIND AND SOUL

"What I give form to in daylight is only one percent of what I've seen in daylight."

—M. C. ESCHER

"Just a non-artist in the art world."

—ROBERTA SMITH, *NEW YORK TIMES* ART CRITIC

*"The most terrible experience for us artists is when a viewer at an exhibition stops for
a half of a second in front of our work and then walks on to the next one. This is
impossible in front of a print by Escher. And usually I feel, when I see his work in an
exhibition or in a book, that after some minutes the picture is not important anymore;
the important thing is the thinking, the mysterium."*

—ISTVÁN OROSZ

M. C. ESCHER WAS born in Leeuwarden, Holland, in 1898, the youngest son of a Dutch hydraulic
engineer. He was a poor student, and the only joy he had in school were his art lessons. When he
was twenty, his father decided that the young Escher should become an architect, so Escher attended the School of Architecture and Ornamental Design in Haarlem. Halfway through his studies, he
decided that his real passion was for graphic arts; but he had to get his father's permission before
he could change course. Escher's father reluctantly agreed to let him change direction.

Escher changed courses and studied with Samuel Jessurun de Mesquita, who was a master print-maker. Mesquita taught Escher how to produce highly proficient woodcuts. For the next seven years, Escher rarely employed any other technique, apart from using pen and ink.

Although Escher was mastering the technique of woodcuts, his work was by no means considered outstanding. The official college report signed by his teachers read, "He is too tight, too literary, philosophical; a young man too lacking in feeling or caprice, too little of an artist." Some years later, Mesquita must have felt a bit of irony when he placed Escher's print "Sky and Water I" on his wall. A family member remarked, "Samuel, I think that is the best print you have ever done."

In 1922 Escher traveled to Italy with two Dutch friends. During this time he took inspiration from the beautiful landscapes of the Italian coast. It was there that his interest in perspective and unconventional viewpoints began to surface. Escher felt at home in Italy and lived there until 1935. During this period he married and had three children.

Each spring, in the company of other artists, he would set off on foot to trek through Sicily, Corsica, and Malta. He would return two months later, tired, but with hundreds of drawings.

Late in life, Escher belittled the Italian landscape prints that he had produced before 1935, describing them as "having little or no value, because they were for the most part merely practice exercises." Nevertheless, without them the later, more famous prints may never have evolved.

In 1935 the political situation in Italy became intolerable to him, and he moved to Switzerland, then to Brussels, and finally set up a permanent home in Holland in 1941.

While in Switzerland, without the southern climate, architecture, and landscapes of Italy, Escher felt bereft of subject matter. He began to look inward and discovered in his mind an even more potent source of inspiration than southern Italy. In 1937 Escher began to experiment with tessellating and morphing figures, and tiling the visual plane. This was to become his predominant style until 1945, and he made hundreds of drawings of tessellating figures. His 1938 woodcut "Day and Night" is perhaps the most famous and admired example of this technique. In addition, Escher became pre-occupied with the notion of two-dimensional figures transforming into three-dimensional ones, as in his 1943 print "Reptiles."

In 1946 Escher began focusing on making unconventional perspective prints. This pursuit occupied him until 1956, when he started to explore the concept of infinity with hyperbolic plane tessellations, such as "Circle Limit IV."

It was during this time that Escher started investigating impossible figures, the result of an inspiring cross-fertilization between a mathematician and an artist. In 1954, the English mathematician Roger Penrose attended a conference of mathematicians, which included Escher's first important exhibition. Up until then, Escher's work had been devoted primarily to tiling the plane and depicting odd structures that appeared to defy gravity. Escher had not yet created any impossible figures.

Penrose had never heard of Escher, who in 1954 was not well known. Penrose, however, was absolutely intrigued by Escher's work, and went away inspired to do something of an impossible nature himself, but that would differ from Escher's own creations. Penrose started experimenting with pictures in which the perspective was inconsistent. He gradually worked at the problem until he came up with the now well-known figure of an impossible tri-bar or triangle, which he believed to exhibit the notion of impossibility in its purest form. Penrose showed the figure to his father, Lionel Penrose, a well-known professor of human genetics who enjoyed mathematical recreations and puzzles. Lionel Penrose became deeply intrigued by his son's impossible triangle and began producing all sorts of similar figures of his own, including an impossible staircase that appears to have no bottom or top step as it goes round and round.

The two Penroses couldn't think of what to do with these strange figures but believed that they ought to be published. However, they could not decide to what discipline they belonged. Lionel Penrose knew the editor of the *British Journal of Psychology*, so he surmised that the best chance for getting these figures published was to put them under the heading of "psychology."

The article was eventually published in 1958. Roger Penrose sent a copy to Escher, having acknowledged his exhibition and contributions in it. In the meantime, Escher had produced his first impossible print, "Belvedere," which exhibits a similar type of self-contradictory, illogical structure.

After receiving the Penrose article, Escher was inspired to create various impossible designs of his own, including the now famous prints "Waterfall" (based on Roger Penrose's impossible triangle) and "Ascending and Descending" (based on Lionel Penrose's impossible staircase). Escher was always very explicit about his sources for these two prints. However, in an odd twist of fate, Escher's name became synonymous with the creation of impossible figures, although, in fact, he created only three impossible prints. His oeuvre consists of well over 400 prints (mostly woodcuts and lithographs), and depicts a variety of themes—mostly landscapes and architectural details in his early work, and in his later work, studies of mathematical objects, visual depictions of scientific and philosophical ideas, explorations of perspective, "story prints," and so on, Escher continued working until his death in 1972.

Interviews with M. C. Escher and Roger Penrose can be seen at http://neuro.caltech.edu/~seckel/mod/.

"DAY AND NIGHT," WOODCUT IN BLACK AND WHITE, PRINTED FROM TWO BLOCKS, 1938,
$15^1/4 \times 27^3/4$ INCHES (39 × 68 CM)

Many people believe that this is Escher's masterpiece, and Bruno Ernst, Escher's biographer, has labeled it "the most admired picture of them all." It represents a turning point in Escher's work. The image is symmetrical; in it the Dutch village is in daylight on the left, and its mirror reflection is in nighttime on the right. The geese, which are black on the left, transform to white geese on the right. This is one of the rare works in which Escher depicted a typically Dutch environment.

"Sky and Water I," woodcut, 1938, 17 × 17 inches (43.5 × 43.5 cm)

In this print, which was done shortly after "Day and Night." Escher plays with figure and ground at the center, either fish or bird can be figure or ground. But the white fish melt into the sky as birds rise, while the black birds dissolve into water as the white fish sink and swim.

"REPTILES," LITHOGRAPH, 1943, 13 × 15 INCHES (33 × 38 CM)

Here Escher creates an impression of three-dimensional reptiles coming out of a two-dimensional image, and then transforming back into two dimensions. How two dimensions suggest the third dimension was a theme that Escher explored in many of his prints.

"ENCOUNTER," LITHOGRAPH, 1944, 13 1/2 × 18 1/4 INCHES (34 × 46.5 CM)

This is another example of Escher's playing with the concept of two dimensions transforming into three dimensions. In "Encounter," the light optimist and dark pessimist come out of their plane-tiling space to meet and shake hands.

"HIGH AND LOW," LITHOGRAPH IN BROWN, 1947, 19½ × 8 INCHES (50.3 × 20.5 CM)

Escher's biographer and friend Bruno Ernst wrote of this lithograph that it is "probably the best print in the whole of Escher's work." In it, the viewer sees the same scene from two different perspectives. In the top half, one looks down into a town square. The lower scene offers the same view, but from a completely different perspective. The square-tiled ceiling seen from below serves as a floor when viewed from above. There are even some steps going down, suggesting that you can enter on the ground floor, but if you peer out of a window, you will find yourself looking out of the top floor.

"CONCAVE AND CONVEX," LITHOGRAPH, 1955, 10¾ × 13¼ INCHES (27.5 × 33.5 CM)

In this work, Escher sought to create a complex world where depth cues are ambiguous. The left side of the print is seen from above, the right side from below, and the views are married in the center, which has many ambiguous depictions. Only the lizards, plant pots, and people are unambiguously depicted. Escher struggled with this print for some time, and wrote to Bruno Ernst about it:

> Just imagine, I spent more than a whole month, without a break, pondering over that print, because none of the attempts I made ever seemed to turn out simple enough. The prerequisite for a good print—and by "good" I mean a print that brings a response from a fairly wide public quite incapable of understanding mathematical inversion unless it is set out extremely simply and explicitly—is that no hocus-pocus must be perpetrated, nor must it lack a proper and effortless connection with reality. You can scarcely imagine how intellectually lazy the "great public" is. I am definitely out to give them a shock, but if I aim too high, it won't work.

"Drawing Hands," lithograph, 1948, 11 × 13 inches (28 × 33 cm)

This is arguably the most well-known of Escher's great masterpieces, and its essential concept has often been copied by other artists. Escher was drawn to the illusion of two-dimensional drawings in perspective suggesting three-dimensional objects. He was intrigued by this visual conflict, and expressed the transition in a number of prints, such as this one.

"Belvedere," lithograph, 1958, 18 × 11 1/2 inches (46 × 29.5 cm)

This is Escher's first impossible print. The top floor of the Belvedere, while parallel to the first floor, is turned 90 degrees, and pillars connect back to front in this most strange construction. The sitting man is holding an impossible cube. In the lower left foreground lies a drawing of the cube. Two small circles mark the places where edges cross each other. Escher asks, "Which edge comes at the front and which at the back? In a three-dimensional world simultaneous front and back is an impossibility and so cannot be illustrated. Yet it is quite possible to draw an object which displays a different reality when looked at from above and from below. The lad sitting on the bench has got just such a cube-like absurdity in his hands. He gazes thoughtfully at this incomprehensible object and seems oblivious to the fact that the belvedere behind him has been built in the same impossible style. On the floor of the lower platform, that is to say indoors, stands a ladder which two people are busy climbing. But as soon as they arrive a floor higher they are back in the open air and have to re-enter the building. Is it any wonder that nobody in this company can be bothered about the fate of the prisoner in the dungeon who sticks his head through the bars and bemoans his fate?"

"Ascending and Descending," lithograph, 1960, 10 × 11¹/₂ inches (25.5 × 28.5 cm)

This work by M. C. Escher is based on Lionel Penrose's impossible staircase. If you follow the steps around, you will locate neither the lowest or the highest step. The figures on the steps are monks. Escher drew the staircase in perspective, which would indicate another size illusion. The monks who are descending should appear gradually smaller, and the ones who are ascending should get larger. They don't. Although Escher was usually very exact in his perspective, in this case he was prepared to cheat a little bit. Escher spoke about the plight of the monks, "The inhabitants of these living quarters would appear to be monks, adherents of some unknown sect. Perhaps it is their ritual duty to climb those stairs for a few hours each day. It would seem that when they get tired they are allowed to turn about and go downstairs instead of up. Yet both directions, though not without meaning, are equally useless. Two recalcitrant individuals refuse, for the time being, to take any part in this exercise. They have no use for it at all, but no doubt sooner or later they will be brought to see the error of their nonconformity."

"Waterfall," lithograph, 1961, 15 × 12 inches (38 × 30 cm)

M. C. Escher's famous print "Waterfall," created in 1961, was inspired by Roger Penrose's impossible triangle. Escher actually used three impossible triangles joined together to form the basis of the structure. During preparatory sketches for this print, Escher's original intention was to draw three colossal building complexes. However, while working, Escher realized that falling water could be used to illustrate the impossible triangle in a unique way. The water spills over an edge and draws a wheel. The water then flows away from the wheel through a brick channel. If you follow the course of the water, you will see that it flows downward and into the dirt until it again reaches the farthest and lowest point, which is identical with its highest and nearest point. Therefore, the water is able to fall again and keep the wheel turning.

"CIRCLE LIMIT IV," WOODCUT IN BLACK AND OCHRE, PRINTED FROM TWO BLOCKS, 1960,
16¹/₄ INCH DIAMETER (41.5 CM)

Do you see white angels or black devils? This is a wonderful example of a tessellating figure/ground reversal. It is based on a circle model of the hyperbolic plane, where no points exist on or outside the circle. An infinite number of angels and devils repeat forever, never leaving the confines of the circle. Escher was inspired to create hyperbolic tessellations (his "Circle Limit" prints) after seeing a hyperbolic tessellation of triangles in an article by the mathematician H.S.M. Coxeter.

CHAPTER 6

Shigeo Fukuda

(1932–)

ABSORBI

"We live dangerously in the world that Fukuda fashions. Reassured and satisfied by a first perception, we may be shaken by the second image, which suddenly turns us head-over-heels."
—FRANÇOIS BARRÉ

"Fukuda has effectively created a universal persuasive power by which anyone from any country can understand his message. He presents us with a developed sense of humor through his forms of 'visual scandal' which comprise his own creative originality, visual expression, and power of forms."
—YUSAKU KAMEKURA

Japanese graphic artist Shigeo Fukuda is without parallel in the world of illusionary art and design and is a master of *absobi*—a concept that combines both play and space. His mastery of design and prolific output have earned him an international reputation. His works cover a wide range of media, including illustrations, graphic posters, three-dimensional sculptures, environmental design, and monuments. Many of his works, both two- and three-dimensional, involve optical tricks and illusions, and in this area he has exploited anamorphoses, impossible figures and objects, figure/ground reversals, composite images, shadow sculptures, and accidental alignments.

Fukuda's choice to enter the world of illusion was as much a career choice as a passion, but he once said it was also a means of distinguishing himself from all his "excellent rivals." He wrote, "When I graduated from the university, all these designers were coming from Kansai to Tokyo. I thought about what I could do so as not to lose to them."

His home and studio, located on a typically narrow Tokyo street, is like a great Fukuda monument, but with real-life effects. What appears to be the front door opens to a blank wall. The real door is part of the seemingly blank wall at the left. All the visual tricks in his home and studio elicit an unsettling reaction from visitors: "What is this? Am I seeing things right? Oh, I get it. Okay. Let's go on. That was odd."

Shigeo Fukuda was born in Tokyo in 1932. As a child he always enjoyed drawing and creating things. He wanted originally to become a cartoonist, and won his first prize for cartooning while in high school. He graduated from the Tokyo National University of Fine Arts and Music in 1956 and joined Ajinomoto Co., Ltd. Since leaving the company in 1958 he has been a freelance artist.

His first great international success was a whimsical exhibition of 120 playthings constructed of natural materials entitled "Toys and Things Japanese: The Works of Shigeo Fukuda." It was held in Tokyo in 1965, and later exhibited in New York City in 1967 at the IBM Gallery. Many of the "toys" in this exhibition would come to define Fukuda and his work for decades to come. Since that time he has shown his pieces in countless international exhibitions, and has been the recipient of as many distinguished national and international awards.

SHIGEO FUKUDA, 1998

His daughter Miran, an artist who aggressively challenges conventional notions about painting, has since joined her father. While their creative motivations may differ, their works share certain similarities—humor, a sense of play, and innovative approaches that turn commonsense perceptions upside down.

Fukuda is the author of several books in Japanese on his own artwork and on general optical illusions; they include *Elements of Ideas, Visual Tricks, Shigeo Fukuda Contrived Designs, Illustrick 412, Posters of Shigeo Fukuda, Great Works by Shigeo Fukuda*, and *Trick Art Trip*.

Additional works by Fukuda can be seen at http://neuro.caltech.edu/~seckel/mod/.

SHIGEO FUKUDA, 1985

"MONA LISA'S HUNDRED SMILES," GRAPHIC POSTER, 1970, $40^{1}/_{2} \times 28^{1}/_{2}$ INCHES (103 × 73 CM)

This was a poster for an exhibition of 100 competitive works for Makoto Nakamuru. One "Mona Lisa" was changed graphically in various ways by using several different kinds of photoengraving techniques. This poster uses one of these techniques.

"LEGS OF TWO DIFFERENT GENDERS," SILKSCREEN, 1975, 5 × 28¹/₂ INCHES (13 × 72.5 CM)

Fukuda is internationally renowned as a graphic artist and designer. Lying at the core of many of Fukuda's graphic designs are the fundamental principles of figure/ground relationships, especially ones that are ambiguous. In this work, Fukuda cleverly creates not only an ambiguous figure/ground perceptual reversal, but one that is also simultaneously impossible. This poster was created for his private exhibition at the Keio Department Store in 1975, where he had an early exhibition of his graphic work.

"Symphony 9 in the Downtown" cover for *Monthly Magazine*, 1985

This was the first in a series of portraits of Beethoven's hair that was characteristically changed every year.

"Bonjour, Mademoiselle," bottles, glasses, shakers, openers, 1982,
21 × 25^1/$_2$ × 13^3/$_4$ inches (53 × 65 × 35 cm)

Here you may initially see only a heap of bottles, glasses, shakers, and openers. But once spotlighted, there appears a smiling *Parisienne de la belle époque.*

"Aquarium for Swimming Characters," wood, 1988, 122 × 112 × 97$^{1}/_{2}$ inches (310 × 285 × 248 cm)

Here the shadow of fish (sea beam, sardine, tuna, globe fish, and shark) reveal themselves in Chinese characters. A movie of this sculpture is on the website http://neuro.caltech.edu/~seckel/mod/.

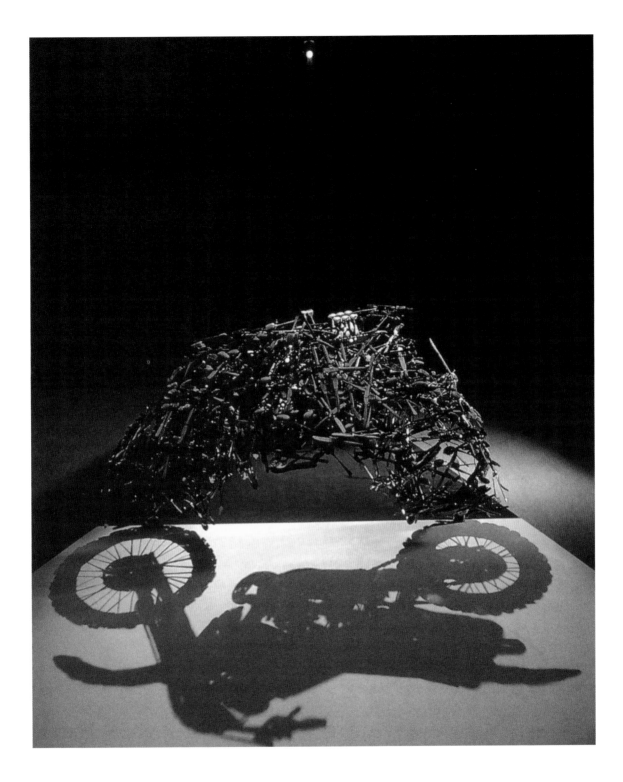

"Lunch with a Helmut On," welded forks, knives, spoons, 1987,
73 × 31 × 42 1/2 inches (186 × 79 × 108 cm)

This shadow sculpture of a motorcycle is built entirely out of 848 welded forks, knives, and spoons. It is based on an earlier concept that Fukuda exhibited in his 1965 show, "Toys and Things Japanese." Fukuda wanted to create a three-dimensional object in which the shadow, as opposed to the actual form, represented the object. Fukuda was to remark that it is extremely difficult to create a three-dimensional object in this fashion that allows light to penetrate evenly. A movie of this sculpture is on the website http://neuro.caltech.edu/~seckel/mod/.

"ONE CANNOT CUT THE SEA," WELDED SCISSORS, 1988, 122 × 112 × 97¹/₂ INCHES (310 × 285 × 248 CM)

After the success of his "Lunch with a Helmut On," Fukuda was commissioned to work on another shadow sculpture. He obtained the rigging plan of the M.S. *Shin-Nippon Maru*, and told his collaborator that he wanted to create an image with metal scissors. There was no response for days. Unbelieveably, however, Fukuda completed the work after only one week. He used 2084 scissors to complete the ship.

"ENCORE," SCULPTURE IN WOOD, 1976, $19^{1}/_{2}$ × $19^{1}/_{2}$ × $11^{3}/_{4}$ INCHES (50 × 50 × 30 CM)

From one angle, the sculpture depicts a pianist, as seen in the top photo. But if you turn it by 90 degrees you will see a violinist, as seen in the bottom photo. The middle photo shows an intermediate point of view, where you can see how the pianist transforms into the violinist. This wood sculpture consists of two silhouettes (the pianist and the violinist) at 90-degree angles to each other. In fact, you can create an endless variety of these silhouette sculptures simply by carefully cutting a block from two different silhouettes at 90-degree angles to each other. Fukuda has made a large number of sculptures using this technique, and his discovery of this principle led to the first incarnation of his work in three-dimensional forms. "Encore" is part of a series of metamorphosing musicians captured at different stages of a concert. A movie of this sculpture rotating is at http://neuro.caltech.edu/~seckel/mod/.

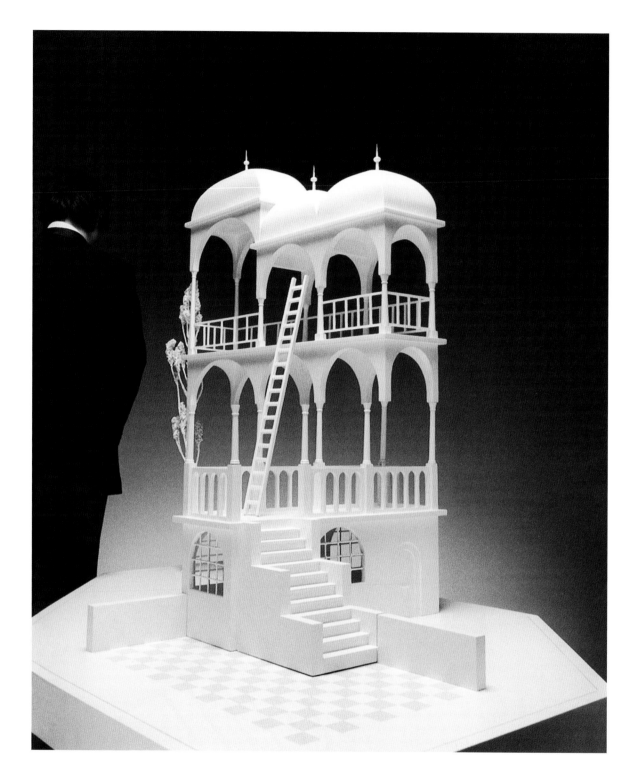

"THREE-DIMENSIONAL MODEL OF ESCHER'S BELVEDERE," SCULPTURE IN WOOD, ACRYLIC PLASTIC, 1982,
43$^{1}/_{4}$ × 64 × 43$^{1}/_{4}$ INCHES (110 × 162.5 × 110 CM)

This is Fukuda's first attempt to sculpt an impossible figure. It is a three-dimensional realization of the building depicted in M. C. Escher's classic print "Belvedere." A movie of this sculpture rotating is on the website http://neuro.caltech.edu/~seckel/mod/.

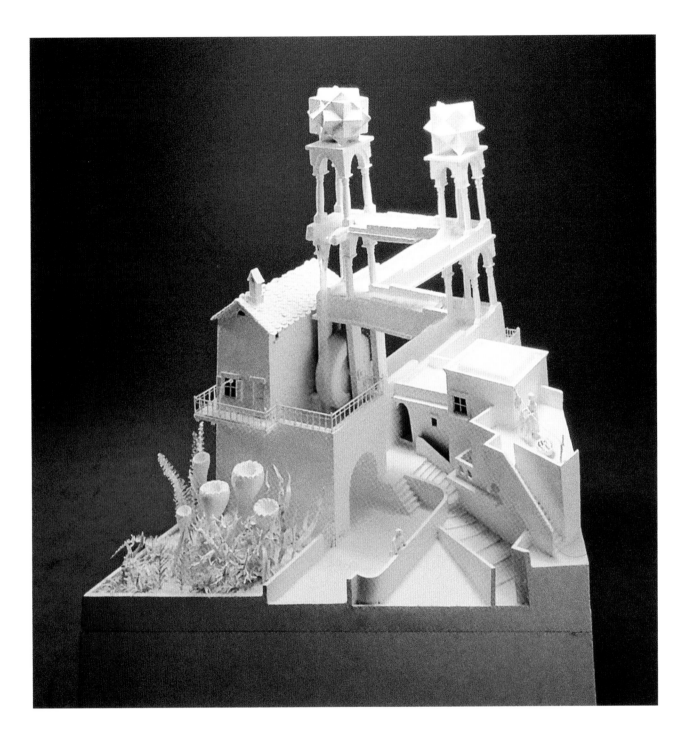

"Three-Dimensional Model of Escher's Waterfall," sculpture in wood, 1985,
59 × 59 × 59 inches (150 × 150 × 150 cm)

This is a physical construction of M. C. Escher's famous print of an impossible building, "Waterfall." This sculpture works with flowing water, which appears to run up the ramp and over the turning waterwheel, only to continue the process in a never-ending cycle of redundant motion. A movie of this sculpture is on the website http://neuro.caltech.edu/~seckel/mod/.

"DISAPPEARING PILLAR," SCULPTURE IN WOOD, 1985

SIDE VIEW OF FUKUDA'S
"DISAPPEARING PILLAR"

This is a physical construction of an impossible columnade, which is based on the classic drawing of an impossible fork. There are three cylindrical columns at the top and two rectangular columns at the bottom. Somehow, they transform into each other. It is only possible to see this impossible configuration from one angle. Viewing this sculpture from any other angle will destroy the illusion. A computer animation of this sculpture rotating is on the website http://neuro.caltech.edu/~seckel/mod/.

"MAIN GATE AT THE 1ST JAPAN EXPO TOYAMA," 1992,
512 × 118 × 512 INCHES (1300 × 300 × 1300 CM)

FUKUDA'S PRELIMINARY SKETCHES
FOR THE MAIN GATE

In 1991 Fukuda was commissioned to design a secure gate for the entrance to the Japan Expo held in Toyama, Japan. Fukuda's design incorporated a visual trick to make visitors wonder which was the real entrance. He wrote, "I have designed a trick, which would stop even those who have a high I.Q. from entering. My interest is how to disorder a human computer. It is like a quiz contest."

FUKUDA'S PRELIMINARY SKETCHES
FOR THE MAIN GATE

"VAN GOGH'S SUNFLOWERS," SCULPTURE IN WOOD,
ACRYLIC, PLASTIC, 1988,
59 × 146 × 80 INCHES (150 × 370 × 203 CM)

"FRESH GUY, ARCIMBOLDO," SCULPTURE IN WOOD,
ACRYLIC, PLASTIC, 1988,
41¹/₄ × 118 × 67 INCHES (105 × 300 × 170)

In the picture frame on the wall is placed a normal mirror. When the manufactured colorful relief is placed on the long, close to three-meter table that is set in front of the mirror, it reflects into the mirror, a perfect and undistorted image of Van Gogh's celebrated "Sunflowers." This anamorphic technique is based on the law of reverse perspective. A movie of this sculpture as seen from different angles is on the website http://neuro.caltech.edu/~seckel/mod/.

Like the previous example, here Fukuda anamorphically presents a distorted version of Giuseppe Arcimboldo's Vertumnus, whose image becomes undistorted when seen in the mirror.

DETAIL OF "FRESH GUY, ARCIMBOLDO"

"CONCAVE AND CONVEX BULLDOGS," 1987

Two bulldogs, whose images are identically reflected in the convex mirror and the concave mirror, are likewise different in their original size and shape.

"Underground Piano," Sculpture in Wood, Acrylic, Plastic, 1984,
47 × 59 × 59 inches (120 × 150 × 150 cm)

If you look in the mirror to the left you will see the reflection of a piano. If you look to the right, you will see a strange construction made out of piano parts, which cast the reflection of a perfect piano when seen from one special angle. A movie of "Underground Piano" is on the website http://neuro.caltech.edu/~seckel/mod/.

SIDE VIEW OF THE "UNDERGROUND PIANO"

FUKUDA'S PRELIMINARY MODEL OF HIS
"UNDERGROUND PIANO"

"MIXED RICE IN CHINESE STYLE," SCULPTURE IN WOOD, ACRYLIC, PLASTIC, 1986

This is the first of a series of Fukuda's "Dishes in the Mirror" series. Fukuda felt that it was quite amusing that the image in the mirror should look more "delicious" than the original.

"MINUTE STEAK," SCULPTURE IN WOOD, ACRYLIC, PLASTIC, 1986

"LUNCH BOX WITH PORK SAUTÉ ON TOP OF GREEN PEPPER MARINATED, FRIED WHITE FISH, STIR-FRIED VEGETABLES, KELP-ROLLED SPINACH IN DRESSING, ROLLED PANCAKE EGG, MOLDED RICE," SCULPTURE IN WOOD, ACRYLIC, PLASTIC, 1986

CHAPTER 7

Rob Gonsalves

(1959–)

MAGIC REALISM

"I believe that there is real magic in life. Sometimes the experience of it can be dependent on one's point of view. I have come to see the making of art as the search for that point of view where the magic and wonder of life appears not so much as an illusion, but as an essential truth that often gets obscured."
—ROB GONSALVES

ROB GONSALVES IS A highly original artist without peer in the artistic representation of illusionary worlds. Although one can definitely see the influences of René Magritte, M. C. Escher, Remedios Varo, and Chris Van Allsburg in his work, many of the illusionary perspective concepts as well as the "magical style" of presentation are unique to him. Many people have labeled his art as surrealistic, but Gonsalves believes that his work differs from pure surrealism because it is deliberately planned and makes the viewer think. His ideas are largely generated by the external world (which many surrealists try to ignore) and involve recognizable human activities combined with carefully planned illusionistic techniques. Gonsalves tries to inject a sense of magic into otherwise realistic scenes, thereby expressing the human desire to believe in the impossible. As a result, the term "Magic Realism" has been used to describe his work.

In trying to shed some light on the development of his current way of working, and his objectives in creating a painting, Gonsalves has stated,

> Much of my free time in childhood was spent daydreaming and drawing. Usually the subject would be an imagined place. For me, the greatest joy in drawing came from giving form to something that had previously only existed in my head. Gradually, my drawings came to be influenced by another aspect of my personality: my strong aptitude for mathematics. Buildings became my main subject. By age 12 I learned the rudiments of perspective drawing, aided by the architectural texts I would pore over.
>
> In my teenage years my interests shifted more towards the realms of surrealism, symbolism and fantasy in art, literature and even music. The emphasis on the subconscious and imagination intrigued me and pointed the way for the first handful of paintings that I was to produce. These images were dreamlike and enigmatic in the manner typical of surrealism. I did not at this point have the confidence to consider painting to be a career path that I could realistically pursue. My painting activities were essentially put on hold as I studied architecture and worked for some years in that business.
>
> Eventually my desire to create images returned, as my work in architecture had not allowed many opportunities to fully exercise my imagination. I made more time for painting, continuing in a surrealist vein, but with new influences, probably largely due to my architecture experience. I had long been fascinated by the techniques that are employed to show the spatial relationship of objects in two-dimensional representations of the world. As I began painting again I felt the need to make the dreamlike, magical occurrences depicted seem more concrete, as if they could be experienced in the physical world. My first introduction to the work of Magritte helped to crystallize for me the direction that my work was to take. His work "The Human Condition" has a magical effect while being at the same time a straightforwardly realistic image. I had wanted to affirm that magical and wondrous experiences are not confined to the realm of dreams or the subconscious, but rather can be derived from our experience and conscious interpretation of the physical world. Magritte's "magic realism" helped me to see how I could achieve this.
>
> From a technical point of view, my work began to employ various optical illusion devices. At the same time however, I became more focused with regard to what I wanted to express about the subjects that I was depicting. In general, I would say that my work has become primarily a celebration of the wonder of imagination.

When one's imagination is brought to bear on a simple life experience, it can be magical—even transcendent.

Frequently, the desire to express the wonder of imagination is manifested as images depicting children at play. The magical transformation in such images illustrates what is happening in the minds of the characters depicted, who are so absorbed by their activity that what is imagined seems to become real. Often these images will involve the type of illusion device that suggests an impossible (yet convincing) change of scale.

Other sources of inspiration for my images can be found in the various dualities that can be observed in life experience: natural vs. human made, urban vs. rural, light vs. dark, material vs. spiritual, etc. The images that are rooted in these concepts usually employ the device of a metamorphosis from one element to another. However, the techniques of optical illusion in my work are utilized somewhat intuitively. The devices that I use are generated perhaps less scientifically than in the work of artists whose primary concern is the creation of optical illusions for their own sake. For me, the particular subject depicted and its emotional impact is crucial; the illusions are a means to an end and must serve the objectives of the overall conception of the image.

In 1990, after an enthusiastic response at the Toronto Outdoor Art Exhibition, Gonsalves decided to paint full time. In 2003 many of his wonderful paintings were incorporated into a children's book entitled *Imagine a Night*. This highly successful book was followed by a sequel volume entitled *Imagine a Day*. His work continues to be highly sought after.

ROB GONSALVES, 2001

"Unfinished Puzzle," acrylic on canvas, 1991, 30 × 30 inches (76 × 76 cm)

"AUTUMN CYCLING," ACRYLIC ON CANVAS, 1994, 20 × 30 INCHES (51 × 76 CM)

"PULLING STRINGS," ACRYLIC ON CANVAS, 1998, 24 × 30 INCHES (61 × 76 CM)

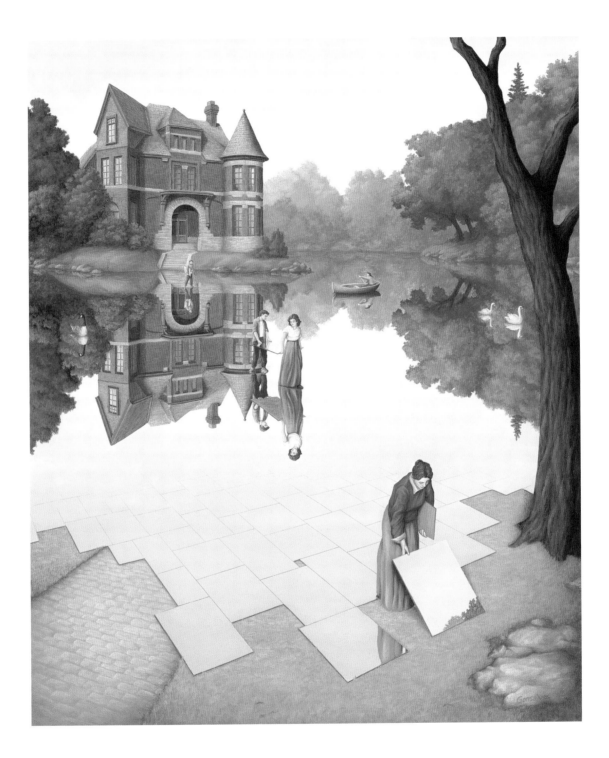

"STILL WATERS," ACRYLIC ON CANVAS, 1994, 20 × 24 INCHES (51 × 61 CM)

"HERE COMES THE FLOOD," ACRYLIC ON CANVAS, 1994, 18 × 24 INCHES (46 × 61 CM)

"Tree House in Autumn," acrylic on canvas, 1995, 20 × 28 inches (51 × 71 cm)

"In Search of Sea," acrylic on canvas, 1995, 34 × 22 inches (76 × 56 cm)

"Cold Comfort," acrylic on canvas, 1996, 34 × 22 inches (76 × 56 cm)

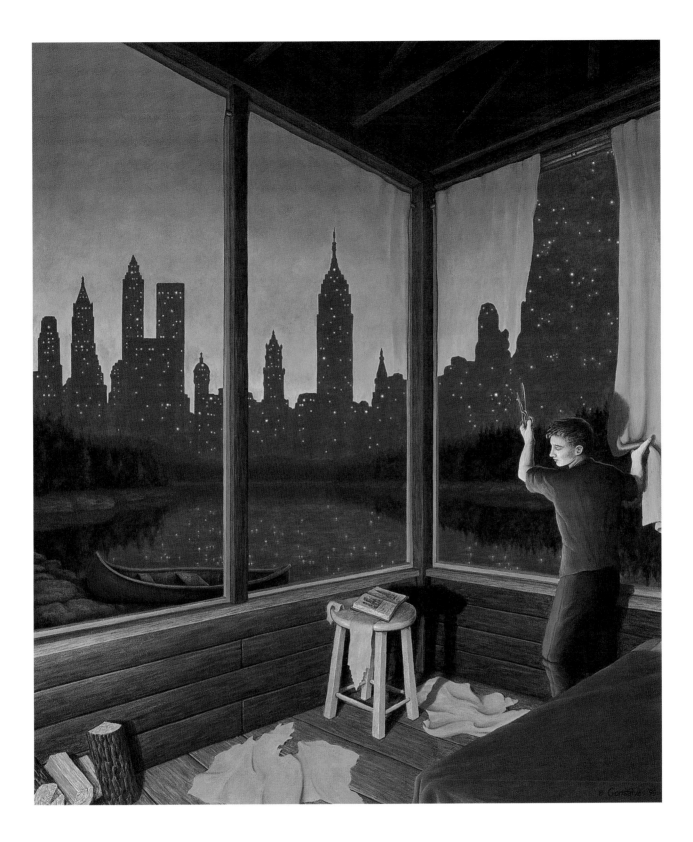

"A Change of Scenery," acrylic on canvas, 1996, 24 × 28 inches (61 × 71 cm)

Outside the windows of the young man's country home, one can see a tranquil setting of a lake, boat, forest, and star-filled night. The young man creates a "change of scenery" by cutting the drapes so that the outline is of an urban city scene. The star-studded night becomes the city lights at night.

"ROOTS AND WINGS," ACRYLIC ON CANVAS, 1997, 26 × 26 INCHES (66 × 66 CM)

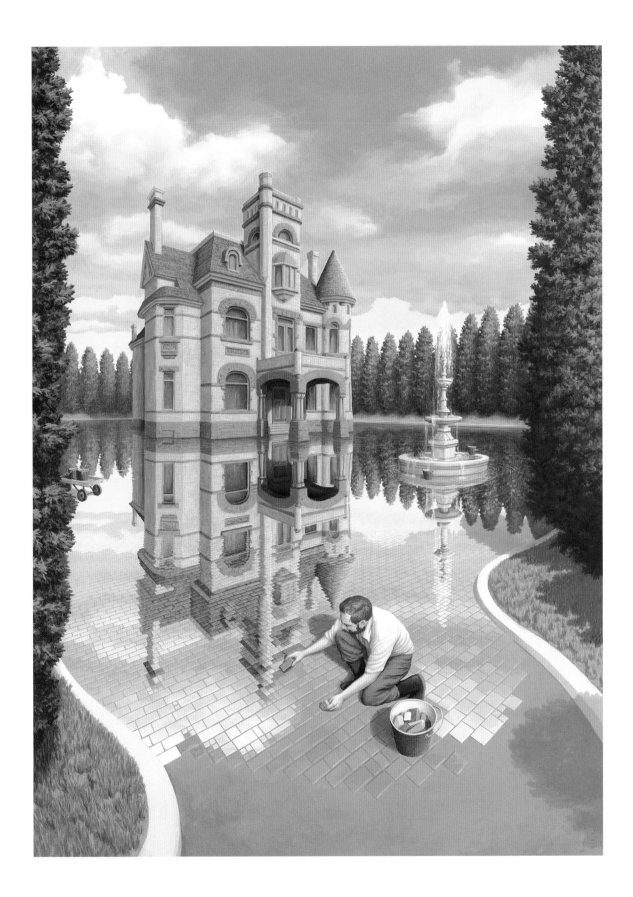

"The Mosaic Moat," acrylic on canvas, 1998, 22 × 30 inches (56 × 76 cm)

"THE NIGHT OF THE LATE NIGHT," ACRYLIC ON CANVAS, 1999, 28 × 24 INCHES (71 × 61 CM)

"THE SUN SETS SAIL," ACRYLIC ON CANVAS, 2001, 40 × 20 INCHES (101.5 × 51 CM)

"Bedtime Aviation," acrylic on canvas, 2001, 30 × 24 inches (76 × 61 cm)

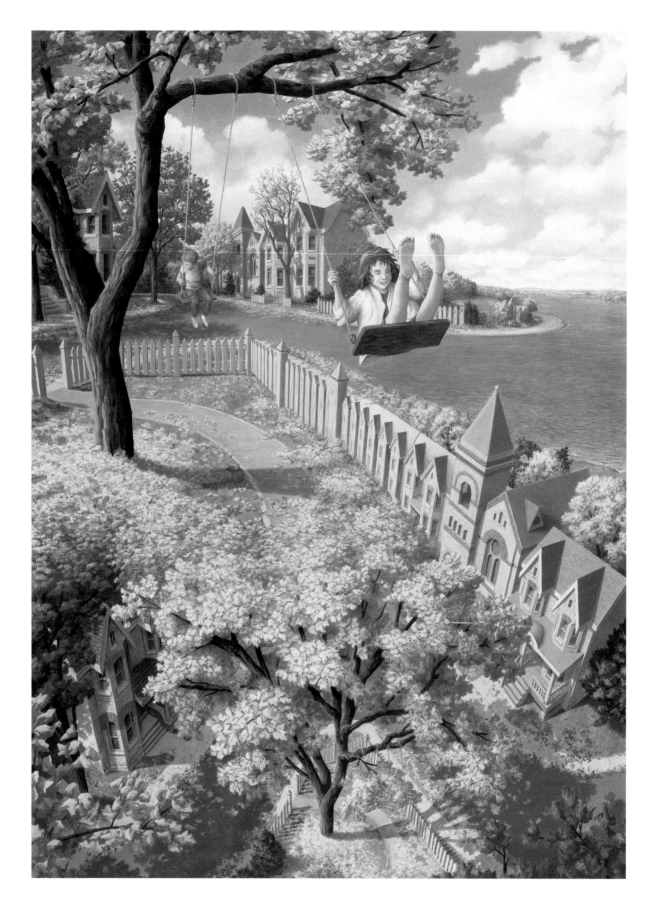

"On the Upswing," acrylic on canvas, 2001, 22 × 32 inches (56 × 81 cm)

Mathieu Hamaekers

(1954–)

OPTICAL CONSTRUCTIVISM

"For me as an artist, it is important that my works are not just a trick or a rational solution of a problem, but that they have a strong aesthetic component."

—MATHIEU HAMAEKERS

BELGIAN ARTIST MATHIEU HAMAEKERS' sculptures really need to be physically seen to be fully appreciated. When you turn the sculpture or walk around it, you will see something totally unexpected. The sculpture transforms itself in a way that you do not expect, leading to a shock or surprise in the viewer, while at the same time remaining a beautiful work of art.

Hamaekers was brought up in an environment that fostered from a young age an appreciation of art and form. His father, a respected carpenter, encouraged him to gain hands-on experience in three-dimensional creativity by building things. His mother strongly influenced his appreciation of aesthetics and the value of form. When he was seventeen, he was deeply influenced by a documentary about the life and work of M. C. Escher, and in particular, his use of the impossible triangle. The next year he decided to pursue a career in art and attended the Academy for Visual Communication and Design in Ghent.

While attending the academy, he created transparent glass structures combined with mirrors as an experiment in perspective. His works at that time showed a deep understanding of perspective, and his talents were immediately recognized. In 1976 he received a National award for Line, Color, and Form for the art he produced at the Academy.

Upon graduation, Hamaekers attended the International University of Lugano. This experience had a tremendous impact on him, and he became deeply intrigued by conceptual and minimal art. It was also at this time that he started to develop his own art form, which he called "Optical Constructivism." During this period, his mind kept being drawn back to the impossible triangle and to other impossible figures. He wanted to see if it was possible to construct these figures in three dimensions. Yet he did not want only to work out an optically correct shape but to build a structure that would be aesthetically pleasing as well. Over the next few years, he developed a mathematical system of projective geometry to hone the shape of these types of structures in three dimensions.

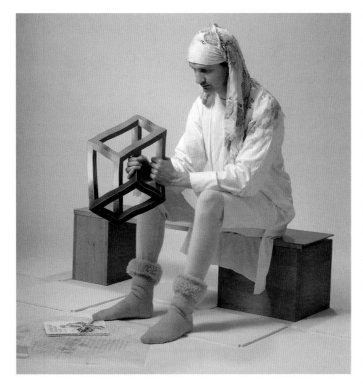

Hamaekers holds an impossible cube, which is based on the figure in M. C. Escher's print "Belvedere," in 1985. A movie of this sculpture rotating is on the website www.neuro.caltech.edu/~seckel/mod/.

He made use of lines, curves, and forms to allow for the most minimal representation of the idea behind the form—not only in its structure, but also in its material. No ornament except color was used. As stated, "It is using this new geometry that I could find new structures, new sculptures that were unimaginable before. My sculptures represent form in its purest essence, and may be the basis for a better and more beautiful form of world."

His first impossible sculpture was based on the impossible cube found in M. C. Escher's print "Belvedere." It was made from colored paper, which at a specific viewing angle would project the image of an impossible cube made out of straight edges, but from any other would reveal its true shape.

Hamaekers's sculptures have been exhibited all around the world, and there is a three-meter-high impossible triangle called "Unity," which he constructed in 1995 outside his studio in Ophoven, Belgium.

To see additional works, an interview with Hamaekers, and to experience how his works transform through rotation, please visit the website http://neuro.caltech.edu/~seckel/mod/.

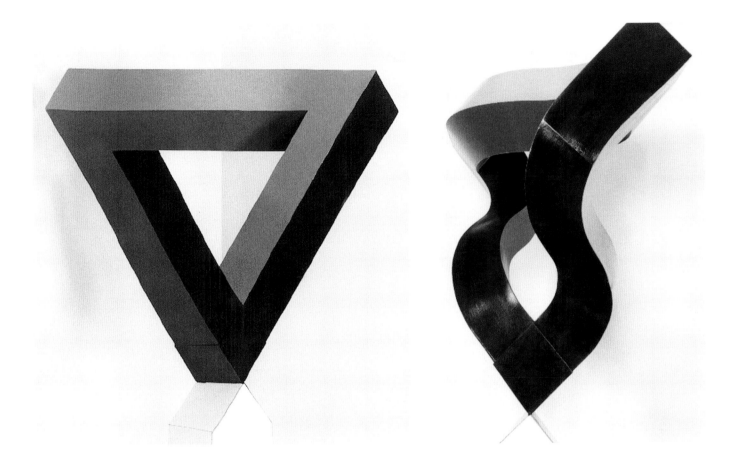

"Impossible Possibility," painted wood and polyester, 1984

This sculpture is based on the impossible triangle by Roger Penrose. From another angle, its true shape is revealed. A movie of this sculpture rotating is on the website http://neuro.caltech.edu/~seckel/mod/.

"IMPOSSIBLE CUBE," PAINTED WOOD AND POLYESTER, 1984

"IMPOSSIBLE
DIAMOND," PAINTED
WOOD, 1984

THE SCULPTURE IS TURNED TO REVEAL ITS
TRUE SHAPE.

"GEOMETRICAL LOVE," PAINTED WOOD AND POLYESTER, 1989, $35^{1}/_{2} \times 31^{1}/_{2} \times 11$ INCHES (90 × 80 × 28 CM)

A movie of this sculpture rotating is on the website http://neuro.caltech.edu/~seckel/mod/.

The World's Premier Optical Illusion Art Brand

"IllusionWorks Logo," 1997

Hamaekers designed this logo for IllusionWorks at the request of the author in 1997. It is an incredible design, incorporating several illusions simultaneously. The impossible triangle also contains the initials "ILW" (IllusionWorks), and the letters are mirror-symmetrical. In addition, the lettering has ambiguous shading, so it can be perceived as both concave and convex.

CHAPTER 9

Scott Kim

(1955–)

AMBIGRAMS

"Scott Kim's Inversions *is one of the most astonishing and delightful books ever printed."*
—MARTIN GARDNER

"Scott Kim has perfected a personal art form—one with grace, elegance, subtlety, and surprises. He draws on a deep understanding of letter forms and visual perception, and the resulting designs are highly original and gratifying"
—DOUGLAS R. HOFSTADTER

AN *AMBIGRAM* IS A word or words that can be read in more than one way, or from more than a single vantage point, such as right side up and upside down. Although it has long been known that certain short words, such as Mom and Bob, have symmetrical properties that can be amusing, it was American graphic and puzzle designer Scott Kim who brought this art form to spectacular heights by creating and designing wonderful letters and alphabets that were able to use rotational and reflectional symmetry. His creations were so beautifully designed that the noted science fiction author Issac Asimov called him "the Escher of the Alphabet." Kim would later agree, he stated,

My work is like Escher's in many ways, except that I work with typefaces instead of natural forms. I too set myself elaborate formal challenges, then let the process of visual problem solving guide me into uncharted visual waters. As a print artist, Escher worked with the most basic elements of black and white, line and form, producing work in multiple editions for a wide audience. I work with the stark black and white forms of type, producing work for print, video and software. Like Escher, my work often veers into the realm of graphic design; I often produce work for titling and illustration.

While many ambigrams are verbally symmetric (the word reads the same in both directions, like "mom"), verbally asymmetrical ambigrams (the words are different, like "mom" and "wow") allow the ambigrammist to include a double meaning in the design. In addition, a large number of words have *reflective symmetry*. This term refers to words that can be read normally, and reflected from a mirror. Working with typefaces creates challenges different from working with natural forms. Kim writes,

> Typefaces bridge the worlds of words and the world of images. Names are especially rich subjects for visual treatment, since we identify them so closely with people. Escher produced several works that played visual tricks with language, but he never pursued it deeply.

Kim was born in 1955 and raised in Los Angeles, where in his teens he began designing and creating highly original mathematical puzzles, a number of which were discussed in Martin Gardner's Mathematical Recreations column in *Scientific American*. Kim was accepted into Stanford, University, where he received a bachelor of arts in music and earned a self-designed Ph.D. in Computers and Graphic Design. It was also during this time that he developed an interest in the use of computers for designing typefaces, a field pioneered by his friend and mentor at Stanford, Donald Knuth. Kim's interest and passion for design and typeface led him to experiment with unusual letter formations that displayed various mathematical and unexpected symmetries.

For years Kim amused his friends and acquaintances with his unique talents, but remained relatively unknown until he came to the attention of Scot Morris, who in 1979 publicized Kim's creations in *Omni*. Later that year, in Douglas Hoftstader's classic Pulitzer Prize-winning work, *Gödel, Escher, Bach,* Hofstadter acknowledged Kim's substantial contributions in the preface: "Scott Kim has exerted a gigantic influence on me. If anyone understands this book, it is Scott." Both of these publications led to a tremendous and international interest in Kim's work. In 1981 Kim published his creations in his book *Inversions*.

Since then, Kim has been continuing to create his wonderful ambigrams and "inversions." In recent years, he has used computer animation to break free of the constraints of the static page, to produce absolutely delightful results with ambigrams and word play. He has also been employed as an independent game designer and has created some of the most original puzzle-solving computer games ever to reach the market. His other pursuits include creating stunningly beautiful educational dance performances about mathematics. He currently lives in El Granada, California (near San Francisco) with his wife Amy and his son Gabriel, and is the author of a monthly puzzle column in *Discover* magazine.

Dynamic ambigrams and wordplay, as well as an interview with Kim can be seen at http://neuro.caltech.edu/~seckel/mod/.

SCOTT KIM, 2001

"DREAM," 1981

Self-Containment: A dream within a dream. Or is it an expanding dream?

"LEVEL," 1981

Self-Containment: Levels within levels. Level is also a palindrome.

"TRUE/FALSE," 1981

Self-Containment: Kim asks, "Is there truth in every falsity, or is it that every falsity is based on a truth?" The word "True" is in lowercase and "False" is in uppercase.

"FIGURE/FIGURE," 1981

Figure/Ground: This image is all figure and no ground. The spaces around the white "figures" form black "figures."

"ILLUSION," 1989

Figure/Ground: The word "illusion" appears to just disappear.

Inversions

"INVERSIONS," 1981

Rotation. Inversions spells Scott Kim when inverted.

"TEACH/LEARN"

Top-Bottom Reflection: "Teach" reflected in a mirror becomes "Learn."

Upside Down

"UPSIDE DOWN," 1981

Rotation: This word describes its own symmetry.

"IDENTICAL/OPPOSITE," 1981

Joined Words: The top of "identical" joins the bottom of "opposite" to make a one-word oxymoron.

Fractal Branching: Each "E" in the word "TREE" becomes the "T" at the root of a smaller "TREE."

"JOY TO THE WORLD," 1988

Rotation: Created for an annual family greeting card.

"MATHEMATICS," 1997

Rotation: Created for "The Secret Life of Squares," a dance performance about mathematical ideas that Kim helped choreograph and perform with the Schaffer and Stern Dance Ensemble.

"MIRROR," 1981

Left-Right Reflection: This word describes its own symmetry. Notice how the dot at the vanishing point has been placed ambiguously on the "i".

"DYSLEXIA," 1981

Left-Right Reflection: A person who is dyslexic often confuses left and right.

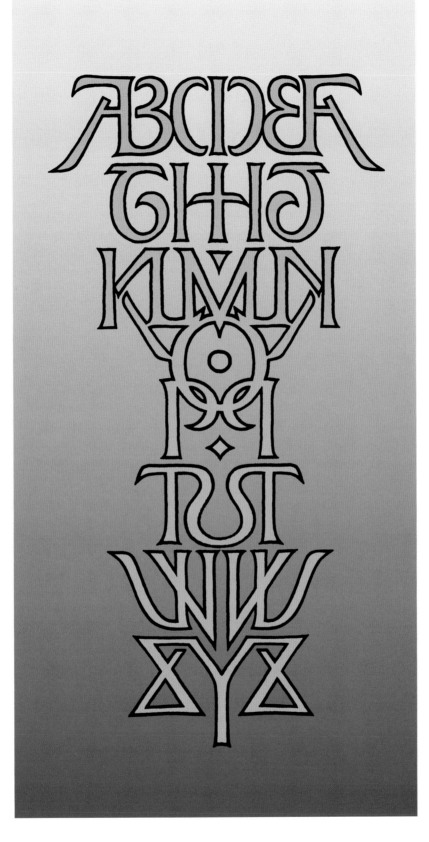

"Alphabet," 1985

Left-Right Reflection. The alphabet has the property that line breaks can be inserted at any point, which you cannot do with words.

"GARDNER," 2002

Crossing Words. Created for the fifth Gathering for Gardner, honoring science and mathematics writer Martin Gardner. The "G" at the beginning of each "Gardner" becomes an "R" at the end of another "Gardner," and every "N" is also an "R."

"M.C. ESCHER," 1981

Crossing Words. This repeating tessellating design contains "M. C. Escher" reading in four different directions. Notice that "M" becomes "E" and "S" becomes "H." Escher himself created several works that feature similar crossing words.

CHAPTER 10

Akiyoshi Kitaoka

(1961–)

ILLUSION OP ART

JAPANESE VISION SCIENTIST AKIYOSHI KITAOKA is a master of optical art. He has extensively studied visual illusions, including geometric ones, light illusions, color illusions, relative motion illusions, and stereoscopic illusions, and has incorporated many new effects into his artistic pieces, creating startling results. Kitaoka views himself as a "self-styled" optical illusion artist. His creed is "a good optical illusion figure (that which gives the largest amount of optical illusion) is beautiful."

Many of his works have been published in Japan under the titles *Trick Eyes* and *Trick Eyes II*. All you have to do to see these wonderful effects is to move your eyes around the image. Most of them work best using peripheral vision, but unfortunately many of the effects also lose their impact when printed, as it is difficult to perfectly control the luminance values in the four-color printing process. It is best to see them displayed on his website, which is listed at the back of this volume.

Akiyoshi Kitaoka was born in 1961 in Kouchi Prefecture, Japan. In 1984 he received his bachelor of science degree in biology from the College of Biological Sciences Second Cluster of Colleges, and then transferred to the University of Tsukuba, where he received his Ph.D. in neuroscience in 1991. He received the Kamitake Gakujutsu Prize from the same in 1998. Kitaoka is now Associate Professor of Psychology at the College of Letters, Ritsumeikan University, Kyoto, Japan.

Additional works by Kitaoka can be seen at http://neuro.caltech.edu/~seckel/mod/.

AKIYOSHI KITAOKA, 2002

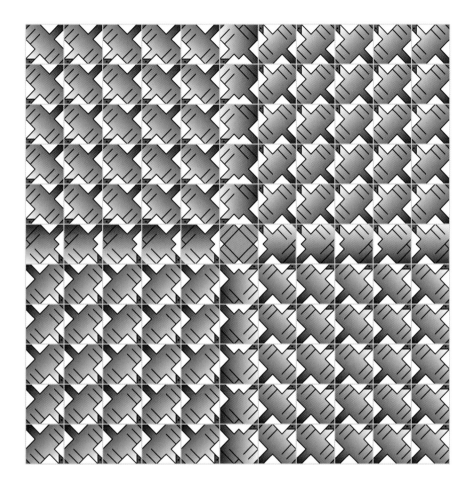

"Café Escher," digital art, 1996

The vertical and horizontal lines are perfectly straight, although they appear bent. This is an example of a twisted-cord illusion.

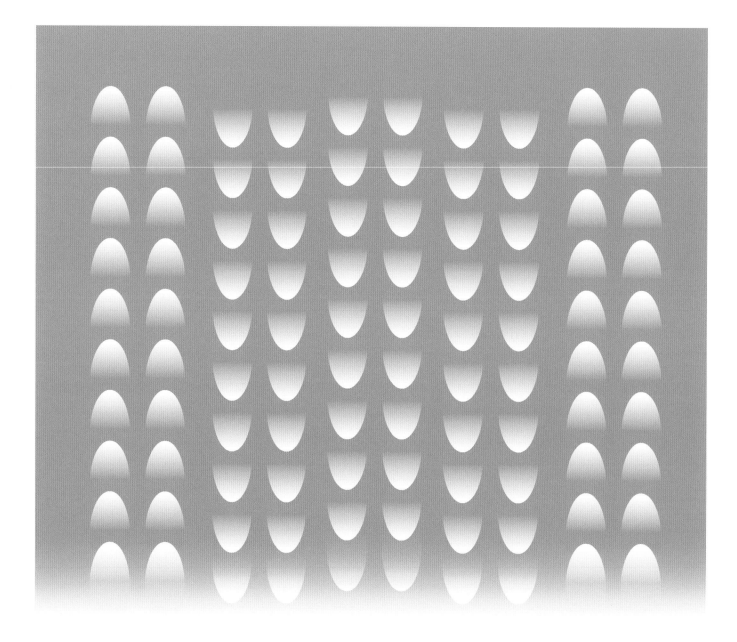

"FALL," DIGITAL ART, 2003

If you move your eyes around this image, the middle section appears to drift downwards, and the two outer sections appear to drift upwards.

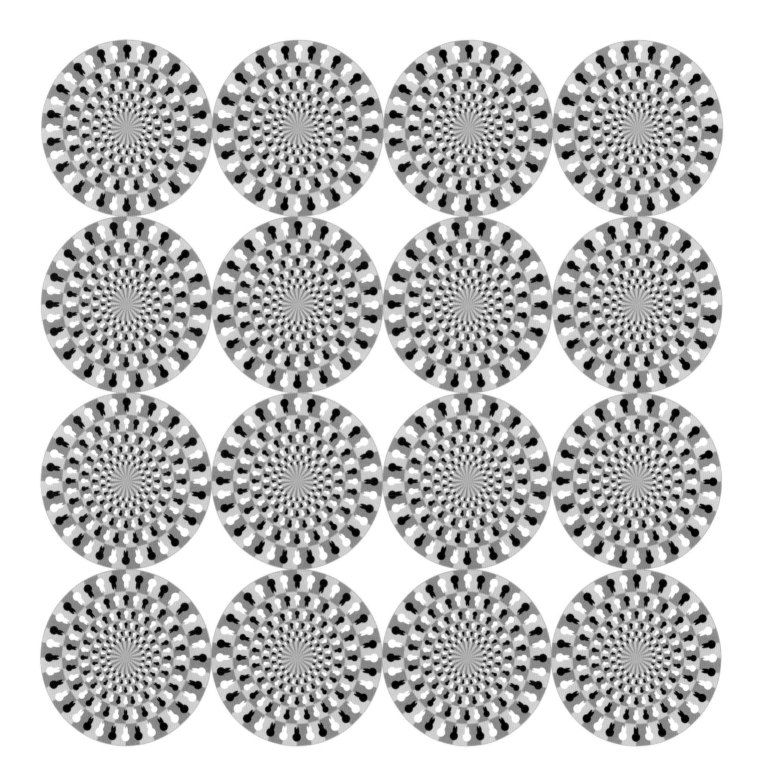

"Rabbits," digital art, 2003

The circular wheels appear to rotate when seen in one's peripheral vision.

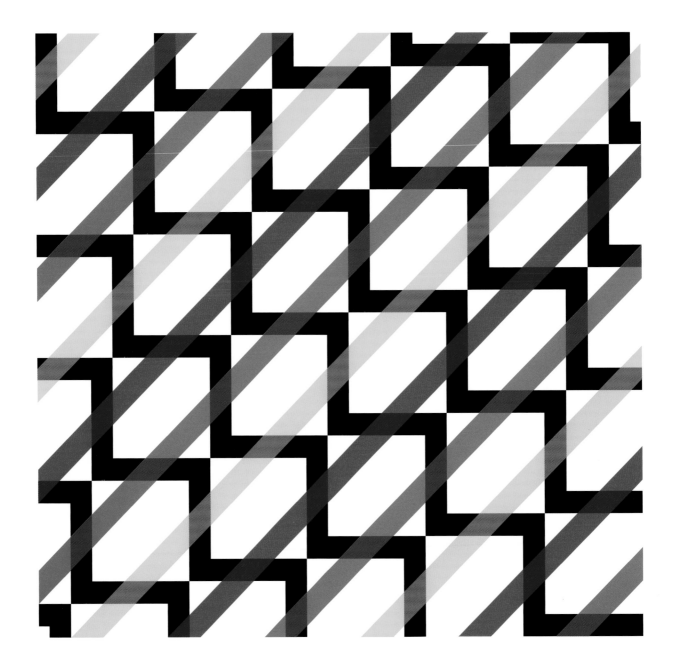

"TAPES," DIGITAL ART, 2003

The diagonals, which appear wavy, are in fact perfectly straight.

152 | MASTERS OF DECEPTION

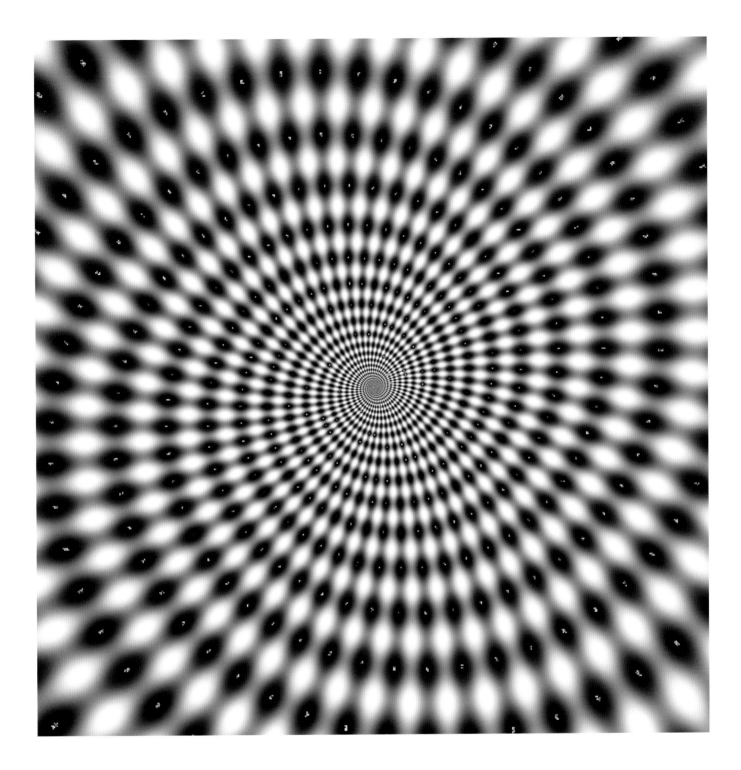

"WARP," DIGITAL ART, 2003

Slowly move your head towards and away from the image and it will appear to zoom in and out.

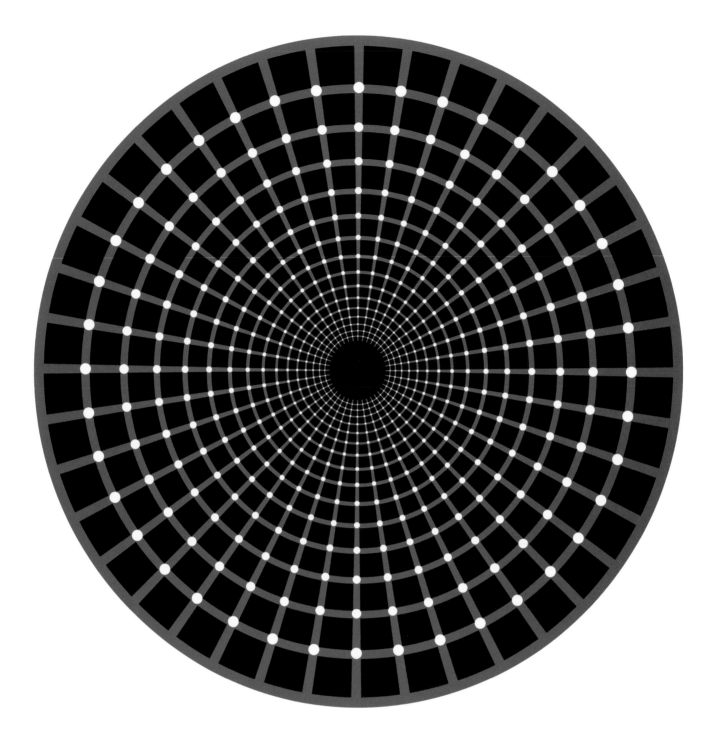

"MUSIC," DIGITAL ART, 2003

Move your eyes around the image and you will see flashing dots; stare at the center and they will all disappear. This is a quirky variation of the Scintillating Grid Illusion discovered in 2002 by American vision scientists Michael Levine and J. Jason McAnany. It is a complex perceptual effect that occurs only under specific circumstances. It may be related to other forms of "visual disappearance" and is termed "blanking." What causes the disappearance is not fully understood.

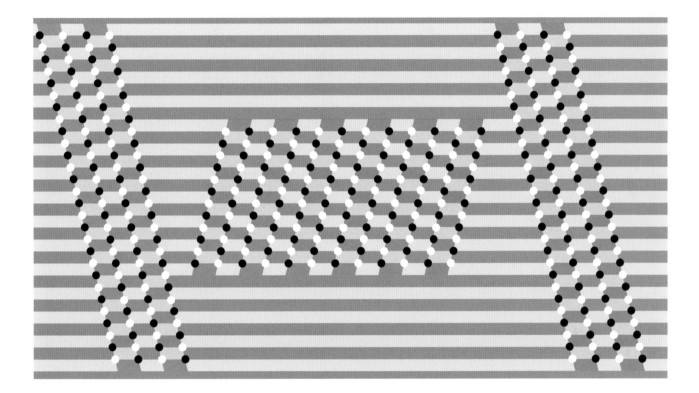

"FERRY BOAT," DIGITAL ART, 2000

The inset appears to drift slightly in the horizontal direction.

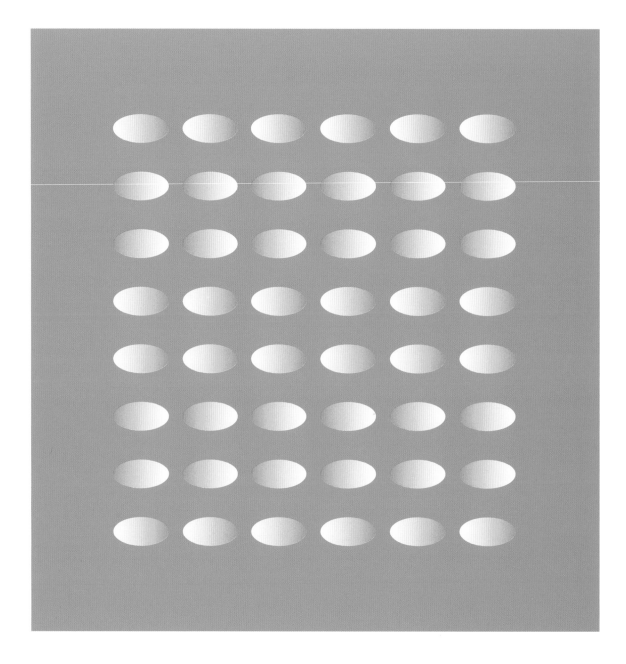

"ANIMALS," DIGITAL ART, 2003

Rows of ellipses appear to move horizontally.

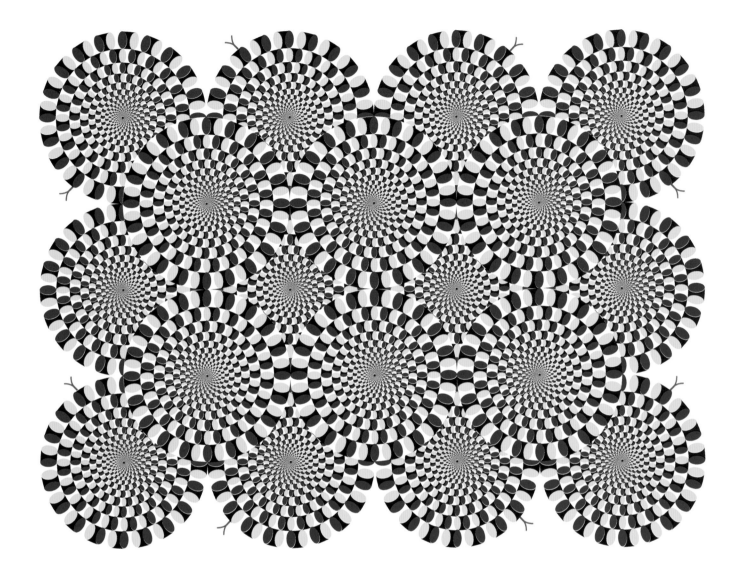

"Rotating Snakes," digital art, 2003

Circular snakes appear to rotate "spontaneously."

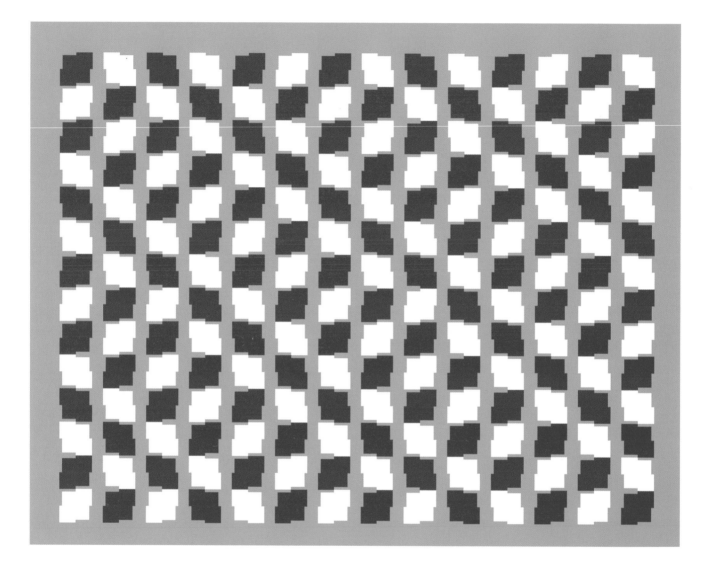

"SEAWEED," DIGITAL ART, 2003

Although the blocks are aligned vertically, the figure appears to show curves.

"Seahorses," digital art, 2003

The left ring of seahorses appears to rotate clockwise while the right one goes counterclockwise.

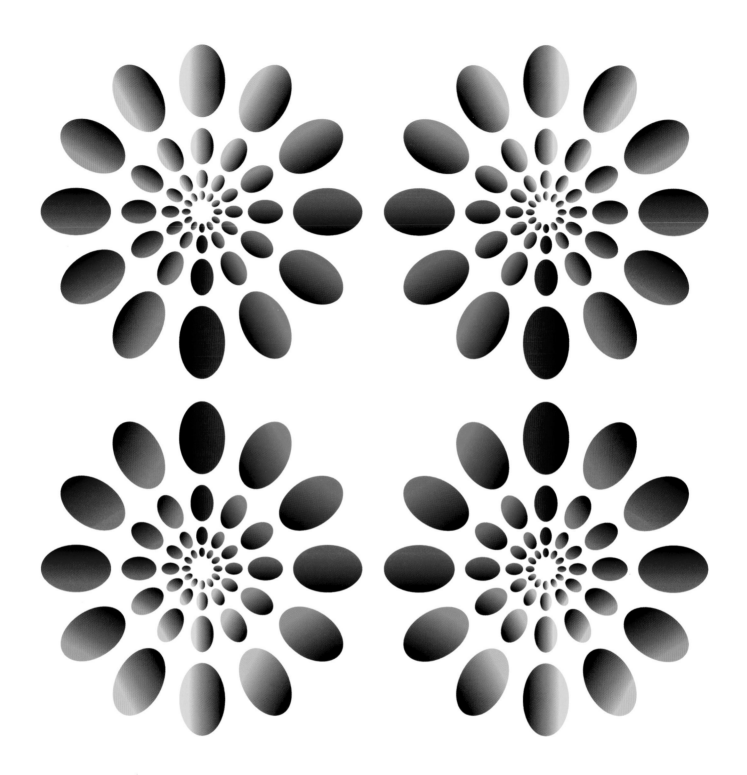

"COLOR-COATED CHOCOLATES," DIGITAL ART, 2003

Each ring of chocolate balls appears to rotate clockwise or counterclockwise.

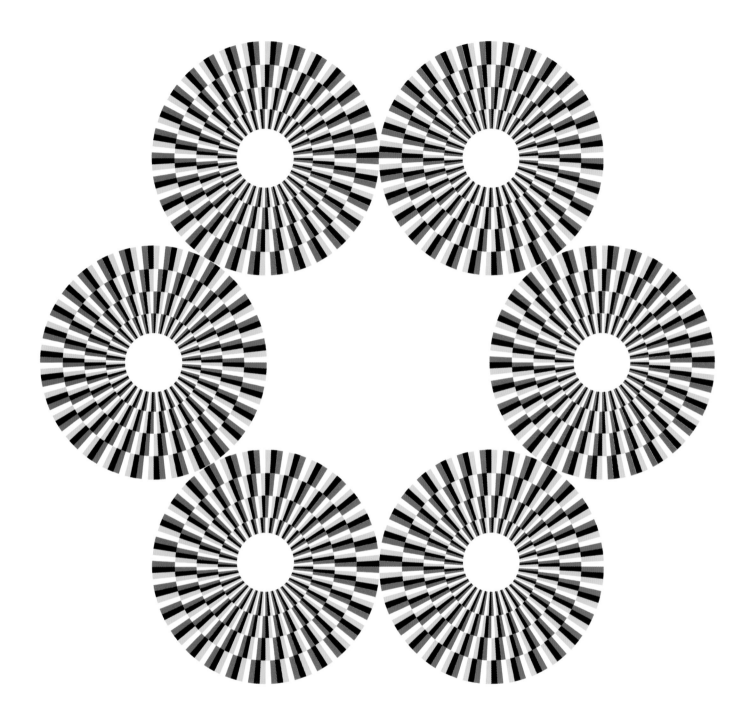

"ROKUYO STARS," DIGITAL ART, 2003

Six white circles appear to scintillate. Moreover, red circles appear to rotate clockwise while blue ones go counterclockwise.

Rokuyo is a week made up of 6 days: *Sensho, Tomobiki, Sembu, Butsumetsu, Taian,* and *Shakko*. Lucky or unlucky days are fixed for each ceremony. For example, a *Taian* day is preferred for weddings in Japan. This illusion is based on the scintillating luster illusion discovered by Bangio Pinna, Walter Ehrenstein, and Lothar Spillman in 2002.

CHAPTER 11

Ken Knowlton

(1931–)

MOSAIC PORTRAITS

"I want to create visual ambiguity—something that demonstrates that recognizable images, especially faces (arguably the most uniformly fascinating of all subject matter) can be made while observing severe or unusual constraints. In spite of such constraints, we are successful at giving meaning to what we see—particularly when recognizing faces. My greatest fun comes from using odd building blocks and stating all constraints explicitly, so that results can be properly evaluated."

—KEN KNOWLTON

COMPOSITE IMAGES CONSIST OF taking disparate smaller views or objects and cunningly arranging them to form a separate and discrete main impression. The sixteentth century Italian artist Giuseppe Arcimboldo was probably the first to create this type of effect.

The American artist Ken Knowlton, who works in a similar vein, creates mosaic portraits from unretouched physical objects or images usually directly related in some way to the person he is depicting. Knowlton usually picks as his subject those people that he personally knows and/or whose works are lives are worthy of respect. In addition, Knowlton has used some of these mediums, such as seashells or dominoes, to create a series of iconic images of people who are easily recognizable. Knowlton creates images that are to be seen from various distances, each of which gives a different a different perception: from far away, most of them are portraits, but at close range each one will be perceived in an entirely different manner, where the close-up geometrical pattern is intriguing in its own right.

Since the 1990s, he has been using his own specially designed software to help create his images. Nevertheless, he is wary of this computer-aided method. "When approaching an artistic project, I still consider using the computer with some skepticism. My own advice to everyone, myself included, is to use the machine for those parts of planning and execution if and where it helps; remember that the important things are not the machines, but the artistic goals, and/or what might be learned or demonstrated—about images—or about human perception and experience. These methods should be used selectively, delicately, modestly, and non-intrusively—letting the artist's goals steer the process."

Knowlton started his career in engineering physics and received a degree from Cornell University. Later he received a Ph.D. in Communications Sciences from MIT, and then worked in the Computing Techniques Research Department at Bell Labs for twenty years. There, in 1963, he developed one of the earliest bitmap graphic systems for computer moviemaking.

"SELF-PORTRAIT IN TRIANGLES," INK-JET PRINT, 2002

Knowlton became interested in creating mosaics on account of a prank perpetrated at the expense of Ed David, a manager working with him at Bell Labs. One day, his friend and colleague Leon Harmon came to Knowlton with a brilliant idea and wanted Knowlton's help in executing it. While David was away, both Knowlton and Harmon snuck into David's office and covered his wall with a picture made of electronic symbols of transistors, resistors, capacitors, and related components. Stepping back from the image, a viewer could see a crude picture of a reclining nude woman. Harmon and Knowlton's plan worked—perhaps too successfully.

When David came back, he was delighted at the joke, but also worried. More viewers than they expected were apparently familiar with the subject matter and could therefore "see" the twelve-foot-wide reclining nude from as many feet away. It was therefore judged an unseemly decoration for the distinguished Bell Laboratory, and was quickly retired. Somehow, smaller versions of the image mysteriously started propagating among lab personnel. Knowlton and Harmon were called into the Lab's public relations department. Officials informed the pair that they could not associate the name of Bell Labs with the nude portrait. Later, in 1967, when the *New York Times* reprint-

KNOWLTON REVIEWS A LAYOUT FOR AN INTENDED PORTRAIT

ed the image (the first time they ever published a nude), the public relations department huddled and decided, so it seems, that since the picture had appeared in the venerable *New York Times*, it was not frivolous pornography after all but "real Art." Their revised statement was, "You may indeed distribute and display it, but be sure that you let people know that it was produced at Bell Telephone Laboratories, Inc."

For Knowlton, this was the beginning of a fascination with composite images that has occupied his eyes, hands, and mind ever since.

Knowlton lives in north-central New Jersey, making art, writing, being a grandfather, and generally keeping a low profile. He can sometimes be coaxed into emerging to speak about his artwork or to join a symposium on art and technology.

Interviews with Ken Knowlton can be found on the website http://neuro.caltech.edu/~seckel/mod/.

"JACQUES COUSTEAU," UNRETOUCHED SEASHELLS AND MISCELLANEOUS BEACH DEBRIS,
1987, 59³/₄ × 48 INCHES (152 × 122 CM)

This portrait of the late famed oceanographer Jacques Cousteau is the first of many seashell mosaics by Knowlton, and was commissioned by the Exploratorium, a hands-on science museum in San Francisco. The portrait consists of seashells and miscellaneous debris (teeth, vertebrae, coral), which were all collected by Knowlton from one small section of beach on the South side of Vieques Island. All the components are unretouched, and essentially all are white. The gray-scale effect is achieved by the percentage occupancy of the local area of the picture.

"HELEN KELLER," SIMULATED BRAILLE (PRINT), 1998, 10 × 8 INCHES (25.4 × 20.3 CM)

Visual (simulated) Braille is used by teachers preparing lessons for the blind. Here, Knowlton used its 64 characters, 16 times each, to portray Helen Keller, the second, and most notable, blind and deaf person to become admirably literate. The picture is based on a photo courtesy of the American Foundation for the Blind, Helen Keller Archives.

"OLD CODERS NEVER DIE THEY JUST FADE
AWAY," KEYBOARDS WITH PAINTED KEYS, 1998,
31 × 25 INCHES (78.7 × 63.5 CM)

This portrait of Bert Hertzog was commissioned in
1998 on the occasion of Hertzog's retirement from his
position as Editor in Chief of Computer and Graphics
Applications. Each key is in its original black or beige,
or painted a solid color.

SETTING KEYS FOR BERT HERTZOG'S
PORTRAIT

"God Does Not Play Dice With the Universe," unretouched dice, 1999

In a famous argument about the probabilistic nature of quantum mechanics with the Danish physicist Neils Bohr, Albert Einstein remarked, "God does not play dice with the universe." This portrait consists of 999 unretouched dice. The number six dieface, however, is not used.

THOMAS KINKADE, "ROSE GATE,"
PUZZLE, 1996, 31 × 25 INCHES
(78.7 × 63.5 CM)

Popular American contemporary artist Thomas Kinkade is known as "the Painter of Light." Kinkade licensed his work "Rose Gate" to an American puzzle company. In the image above, the puzzle pieces are correctly arranged, but not joined together. Knowlton, using another copy of the same puzzle, sorted all of the individual puzzle pieces according to light, color, and value.

"THOMAS KINKADE REVEALED," UNRETOUCHED PUZZLE PIECES, 1999,
31 × 25 INCHES (78.7 × 63.5 CM)

After Knowlton had sorted the puzzle pieces, he rearranged them, against a black background, to form the portrait of Kinkade. In this way, the artist was discovered in his own work.

SETTING THE PUZZLE PIECES FOR THE
PORTRAIT OF THOMAS KINKADE

"PORTRAIT WITH A SINGLE LINE," SPACE-FILLING CURVE, INK-JET PRINT,
2000, 8 × 8 INCHES (20.3 × 20.3 CM)

This is a portrait of Douglas McKenna, who discovered several families of strictly tiling, self-avoiding, space-filling curves. Be sure to look at the portrait from a distance, and then as closely as you can. It is composed of 38,291 straight-line segments joined at right angles. The portrait is based on the photo by Jef Raskin.

"SPOOLS OF THREAD," COLORED SPOOLS OF THREAD, 2001, 32 × 26 INCHES (81.3 × 66 CM)

This is Ken Knowlton's portrait of, tribute to, and gift to Aaron Feuerstein, the president and owner of Malden (fabric) Mills in Lawrence, Massachusetts. In 1995 a devastating fire destroyed three main buildings of the mill complex. However, instead of collecting the insurance money and closing up shop, Feuerstein kept workers on salary during the recovery. His response to the situation has been widely acclaimed as a stellar example of decency in business.

Knowlton's portrait consists of 945 inch-long multicolored spools of thread alternately oriented vertically and horizontally. They give the impression, from intermediate distances, of woven fabric. This artwork, therefore, has three levels of interpretation: a portrait, a woven fabric, and spools of thread.

BOXES OF COLORED THREADS USED TO CONSTRUCT THE PORTRAIT OF FEUERSTEIN

USING COLORED THREADS TO CONSTRUCT THE PORTRAIT OF FEUERSTEIN

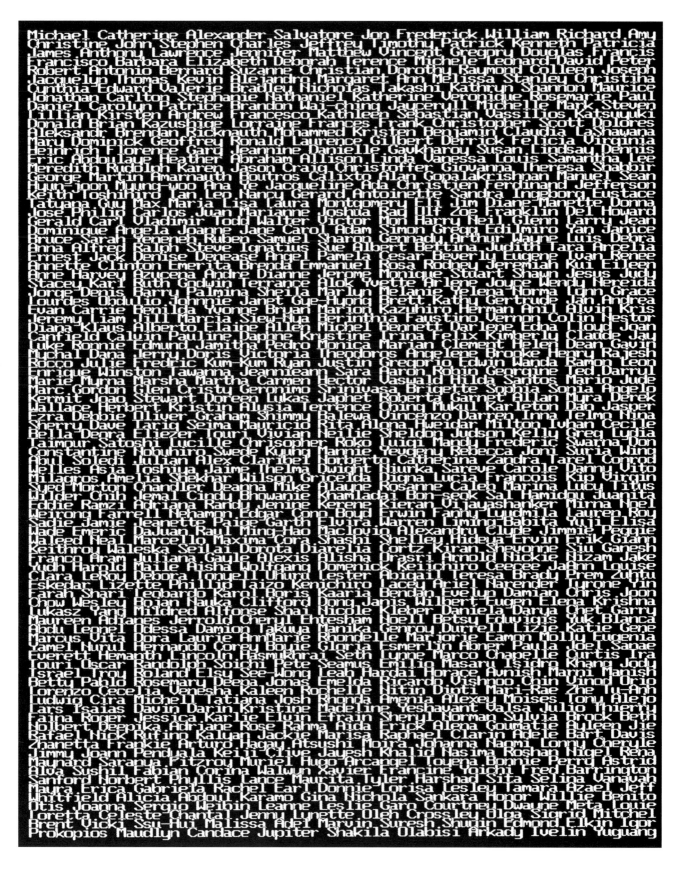

"In Memoriam—9/11," ink-jet print, 2002, 10 × 8 inches (25.4 × 20.3 cm)

A phantom World Trade Center and the first names of the victims of the attacks on September 11, 2001.

Mathematician Solomon Golomb is the popularizer of mathematical tiling known as polyominoes. Polyominoes are a collection of squares joined together along their edges. They have inspired popular video games like Tetris, and have contributed to the study of combinatorial geometry and tiling theory. Knowlton's portrait of Golomb was created using pentominoes (each pentomino shape consists of five squares, and there are twelve different pentomino shapes). Each pentomino shape was used twenty-seven times to create the final image.

"CARD MAGIC," SIMULATED CARD SYMBOLS (PRINT), 2002, 10 × 8 INCHES (25.4 × 20.3 CM)

Swedish magician Lennart Green is one of the world's leading card magicians. His portrait consists of various symbols and numbers from a deck of playing cards.

"Puzzle Master," tangram pieces (print), 2002, 10 × 8 inches (25.4 × 20.3 cm)

Jerry Slocum is a leading authority and collector of mechanical puzzles. This portrait, created in 2002, is made out of tangrams, which are the shapes of a classic Chinese dissection puzzle, and are always combined in some fashion to form interesting and elegant figures. A tangram figure involves the same, standard set of seven pieces. This portrait uses thirty-two sets of pieces.

"WILL SHORTZ,"CROSSWORD PUZZLE GRID, 2003, 10 × 8 INCHES (25.4 × 20.3 CM)

Widely known for his puzzles, Will Shortz has for many years been the crossword editor of the *New York Times*. This puzzle grid observes many (but not all) of the traditional rules of grid construction. Amazingly, it has been completed, with words and their clues, by crossword puzzle expert Frank Longo, a longtime contributor to the *New York Times*.

Guido Moretti

(1947–)

T RANSFORMING S CULPTURES

"I like to think of my latest sculptures as strange objects wandering through space,
rotating around themselves in a dimension in which the concepts of 'up, down, in, and
out' are totally meaningless."

—G UIDO M ORETTI

G UIDO M ORETTI'S T RANSFORMING S CULPTURES are an incredible experience to behold. They are paradoxes within a paradox. Not only do they appear to violate physical reality with their illogical structures, but they also present another surprise to the viewer. As the sculpture is turned, it radically transforms itself from one impossible shape into another, which seems in itself to be a paradox.

Moretti's sculptures violate a viewer's expectations about shape constancy, that is, the tendency of one's perceptual system to keep consistent the true shape of objects as they are viewed from different angles. Experience "shapes" one's expectations of how an object should change as one moves around it. His sculptures are masters of camouflage, hiding hidden structures that are revealed only from another angle—Nature has never been this devious.

Moretti's sculptures have their greatest impact when seen in person, and when the sculpture is slowly rotated (or the viewer can move around the sculpture). There is always a noticeable gasp from the audience as the sculpture radically transforms from one shape into another. Many of his designs are based on the impossible figures created by the Swedish artist Oscar Reutersvärd, though Moretti also makes use of other classic illusionary forms.

Moretti lives and works in Bovezzo, just outside Brescia, Italy. He was born in 1947 in Gardone, Italy where his father was a carpenter and used part of the hallway of the house as his workroom. Having grown up surrounded by wood, Moretti was always fascinated by the material: "You breathe it, it gets inside you—the colors, the smells! I've still got the smell of glue in my blood." He much preferred his father's carpentry shop to school, and let his imagination run wild while playing with wood and plaster. It was in this atmosphere that his first sculptures took shape.

Despite his passion for woodworking, Moretti decided to pursue a career in the sciences. He enrolled at the Zanardelli Technical Institute and later at the Brescia Technical Institute. It was while studying science that he became captivated by the beauty of analytic geometry. He continued his academic studies at Padua University, while furthering his artistic pursuits. After graduating, he started teaching physics but continued to be involved with various artistic groups.

GUIDO MORETTI, 2003

Moretti's adventure as a sculptor began with experience in figurative portrayal that lasted fifteen years, while he was studying for a degree in physics. After this experience, his two souls—the scientific and the irrational—found the right point of contact in search of rules and laws that govern the birth of shapes. The first two methods he applied were stratification and rotation. His latest innovative method is called *orthogonal intersections,* in which solutions come in the form of rotations and sculptures are made on the basis of variable geometry. It consists of cutting the material following well-defined lines drawn on two faces of a cube or parallelepiped. He observes, "It is clear that my scientific training has had a profound effect on my formation of ideas and aesthetic inventiveness, but artistic intuition springs only from an exciting blend of rationality and emotion."

Additional works by Moretti can be seen at http://neuro.caltech.edu/~seckel/mod/.

"Cube to Non-Cube," cast bronze, 1997, $10^{1}/_{4} \times 8^{1}/_{2} \times 12^{1}/_{4}$ inches ($26 \times 22 \times 31$ cm)

The photographs show three different views of the same sculpture, which transforms from an impossible triangle to a cube. The far right shows the intermediate view.

"Impossible Pillars to Impossible Blocks," cast bronze, 2000, $3^{1}/_{2} \times 6 \times 9^{1}/_{2}$ inches ($9 \times 15 \times 24.5$ cm)

In the left photo, you will see three vertically aligned blocks at the top, which somehow merge into two vertically aligned blocks on the bottom, forming an impossible configuration. Furthermore, you are able to look through the sculpture to see the blue background.

The middle photo shows the same sculpture turned clockwise by 90 degrees. Now there is a set of several horizontally aligned impossible blocks. Again, you can look through the sculpture to see the blue background, but you do not see the vertical bars from the previous viewing angle!

The far right photo shows the sculpture from an angle midway between the other two angles.

The impossible pillars and blocks are based on impossible figures drawn by Swedish artist Oscar Reutersvärd.

"Invisible Pyramid 1," cast bronze, 2001, $8^1/_4 \times 8^1/_4 \times 7^1/_2$ inches ($21 \times 21 \times 19.5$ cm)

This sculpture depicts a pyramid with illusory contours. The pyramid can be perceived, even though there are no edges to define it. The Italian vision scientist Gaetano Kaniza first described illusory contours.

"Impossible Pillars and Trident," cast bronze, 2001, $4^1/_4 \times 5 \times 11^3/_4$ inches ($11 \times 13 \times 30$ cm)

"IMPOSSIBLE OVAL AND PILLARS," CAST BRONZE, 2001, $3^1/_2 \times 7^3/_4 \times 9^1/_2$ INCHES ($9 \times 20 \times 24.5$ CM)

"AMBIGUOUS TO AMBIGUOUS," CAST BRONZE, 2001, $5^1/_4 \times 5^1/_4 \times 5^3/_4$ INCHES ($13.5 \times 13.5 \times 14.5$ CM)

This sculpture is based on the ambiguous and impossible figure by Thíery, in which the bottom can also be perceived as the top.

"IMPOSSIBLE BLOCKS OF TWO ENTIRELY DIFFERENT CONFIGURATIONS," CAST BRONZE, 2003

The blocks appear to be arranged in an impossible configuration, and the two different special viewing angles present the blocks in their mirrored views.

CHAPTER 13

Vik Muniz

(1961–)

A Change of Medium

"There's something redeeming in using the barest mechanics to produce an image. I don't want to amaze you with my powers to fool you. I want to make you aware of how much you want to believe in the image—to be conscious of the measure of your own belief, rather than my capacity to fool you. You see it, but at the same time you see how it works. I have been called an illusionist, but I have always considered myself a twisted kind of realist."

—Vik Muniz

VIK MUNIZ'S TRADEMARK IS visual punning, and as such, he has become one of the leading artists of the international contemporary art scene. He is known for his use of disparate, nontraditional materials—such as chocolate syrup, sewing thread, sugar, dirt and leaves, dust, garbage, cotton, nails, and even spaghetti marinara—to create his strikingly beautiful and powerful images. He is much more than just "clever": His craftsmanship is impeccable, and his sensibilities are highly refined. Muniz exploits our tendency to draw quick conclusions about what we think we see. His art reminds us of the old adage that appearances can be deceiving, and his mission is nothing less than to "change the way people look at things."

Muniz recreates images that already exist, which are derived from photos or well-known paintings. However, he does not set out to copy the originals, but to conjure up those images strictly from memory so that the connections are not literal, but intuitive. Muniz wants to depict "pictures of thought"; therefore, his work is not that of a copyist or a virtuoso of pictorial memory. His idea is to use existing images as a kind of cover/camouflage for conveying deceptively simple ideas that in fact raise numerous questions and contain several levels of interpretation—to break in, as it were, to the general storehouse of visual memory. As Muniz says,

> The power of the image lies in its ability to be underestimated. They're sweet, simple things. You think you know what you're looking at. What I wanted to do is make images not transparent, but opaque, using these bad actors—soil, sugar, thread—to create a series of layers and make it a little harder for the viewer to get to the subject. In this way you engage the viewer in an analytical relationship to the image that hopefully will work as a vaccine. These images are like little antibodies; they change the perception of all images in their own class.

Muniz does not view himself as much as an artist so much as a photographer.

> I am a photographer because my work ends up being a photo. For example, the Sugar and Soil series have a lot more to do with photography itself: the idea that the image is composed by a certain logical arrangement of tiny dots that we can't perceive individually.

His choice of materials is meant to be provocative.

> I usually choose to work with perishable or unstable materials because I want to emphasize the temporal element in every picture. They are records of short performances, about a second long, enacted exclusively for the lenses of my camera . . . I don't try to attract any attention to the mundane aspect of the materials I use. I just don't discriminate. All materials are good for something in a picture, be it oil paint or elephant excrement. It's interesting how people become amused by a shift in medium.

> Art for me is not about saying things. It's about discovering ways to say them. Basically, I am trying to compound an epistemology of flattened visual forms. All these things, while they remain photographic objects, they attempt to make the viewer examine the role of representation as an exchange and interaction of forms rather than an improvement on a specific one. There's no way to discover without being involved in the making of it, and through the process, you start to realize the mechanics of representation and you start to use them better. I think the end result is just the beginning of a narrative that moves backward in time. For

me, an interesting work of art has to have this quality that when you look at it for the first time, you wonder how it was done.

Vik Muniz was born in 1961 and grew up in São Paulo, Brazil. Although he drew compulsively as a child, he was reared in a working class family, so it never occurred to him to become an artist. He spent his early years doing a variety of menial odd jobs, which were later to become an important influence on his life and work. In Brazil, he studied advertising, and worked for an advertising agency. In 1983, he moved to the United States with the insurance money that he got from an accident—he had tried to intervene in a fight and was shot in the leg. At the time, he could not speak a word of English.

Muniz's early work consisted of sculptural installations, but in the late 1980s, he started to incorporate photography into them. The year 1991 brought a breakthrough, when he created a photographic series called *The Best of Life*, in which he made pencil drawings, from memory, of several world-famous photographs and then photographed his drawings. In 1993 he started a series of photographs of cotton that he had formed into ambiguous, cloudlike forms. He has also worked on large installations in earth, which can only be seen from a vast height. Over the past decade, he has been featured in innumerable international shows, and has been the recipient of as many prestigious awards. Most recently he has been making art that his mother likes, but Muniz admits, "I don't know if this is good or bad."

Muniz lives and works in New York City. An in-depth interview and examples of Muniz at work creating some of his images can be found at http://neuro.caltech.ecu/~seckel/mod/.

SELF-PORTRAIT OF THE ARTIST, FRONT AND BACK, MADE OUT OF MAGAZINE CONFETTI, 2003

"FIAT LUX," TONED GELATIN PRINT, 1994, 20 × 24 INCHES (50.8 × 61 CM)

"RELAXATION," TONED GELATIN SILVER PHOTOGRAPHS, 1994, 20 × 24 INCHES (50.8 × 61 CM)

"The White Shirt," toned gelatin print, 1994, 20 × 24 inches (50.8 × 61 cm)

"The Artist's Shoes," toned gelatin silver photographs, 1994, 20 × 24 inches (50.8 × 61 cm)

"GUANABARA BAY SEEN FROM NITEROI, AFTER MARK FERREZ," GELATIN SILVER PRINT, 1996,
20 × 24 INCHES (50.8 × 61 CM)

Muniz's series of powerful landscapes, utilize the medium of hundreds if not thousands of yards of sewing thread. They developed out of his frustration to properly depict with wire the depth relationships in a landscape. Muniz stated,

> I wanted to try different subjects, but I discovered by changing the material in which I was drawing that each material could only render certain things well. I needed something more fluid, so I began working with sewing thread. The process is very similar to the wire objects except that it allows me to build up the material and create volume. In one hand you have a drawing and in the other you have the photograph of the "actor" responsible for the enacting of that landscape. When you perceive the one, you lose the other. It works like a visual illusion, like the Necker cube or Rubin vase.

Muniz's Pictures of Thread series are not direct copies of the images that inspired them, but were recreated from Muniz's memory of those artistic works. Twenty-four thousand yards of thread were used in this landscape.

"Le Songeur, After Corot," toned gelatin print, 1996, 20 × 24 inches (50.8 × 61 cm)

Sixteen thousand yards of sewing thread were used to create this image.

"Apple Tree, after Alget," toned gelatin print, 1998, 20 × 24 inches (50.8 × 61 cm)

Two hundred yards of sewing thread were used to make this print.

"The Castle at Bentheim, After Jacob van Roysdael," toned gelatin print, 1999,
20 × 24 inches (50.8 × 61 cm)

Twenty thousand yards of sewing thread were used to create this image.

"The Helminghan Dell, After John Constable," toned gelatin print, 1999,
20 × 24 inches (50.8 × 61 cm)

This image comprises eleven thousand yards of sewing thread.

"Church on a Hilltop at Vareerngeville, after Claude Monet," toned gelatin print, 1999,
20 × 24 inches (50.8 × 61 cm)

Nine thousand yards of sewing thread were used to create this image.

"VALENTINA, THE FASTEST," GELATIN SILVER PRINT, 1996, 14 × 11 INCHES (35.6 × 27.9 CM)

Muniz's stunningly beautiful portraits of Carribean children are made entirely out of cupfuls of sugar, where the sugar granules are individually arranged on black paper. They grew out of a very personal circumstance. He was vacationing in St. Kitts with his wife, and every day they went swimming with a group of the local children. Muniz and his wife became quite endeared to the sweet, happy, and unspoiled children, and got to know their names and interests. During the trip they had a chance to visit the sugar plantations where the children's parents worked extremely hard in the scorching sun. The parents' lives were sad and bitter.

Muniz took pictures of the children and brought the photos back to New York, where he would transform them. He wrote,

> One morning, as I was drinking my coffee and looking at the pictures, I remembered this poem by the Brazilian poet Ferreira Gullar in which he is drinking coffee and begins to wonder about the origin of sugar. He ends with a seminal phrase: "It is with the bitter lives of bitter people that I sweeten my coffee on this beautiful morning in Ipanema." The radiant childhood of those children will inevitably be transformed by sugar. I realized they take the sweetness out of the children by making them work in the fields. It's very hard work. All the sweetness of them ends up in our coffee. Children who become sugar—it hit me like a brick.

Muniz tried copying the snapshots onto black paper using the medium of sugar, which he sprinkled over the surface. It was an experiment that, much to his surprise, worked very well.

"Big James Sweats Buckets," gelatin silver print, 1996, 14 × 11 inches (35.6 × 27.9 cm)

"Jacynthe Loves Orange Juice," gelatin silver print, 1996, 14 × 11 inches (35.6 × 27.9 cm)

"Lil Calist Can't Swim," gelatin silver print, 1996, 14 × 11 inches (35.6 × 27.9 cm)

"Valicia Bathes in Sunday Clothes," gelatin silver print, 1996, 14 × 11 inches (35.6 × 27.9 cm)

"SELF-PORTRAIT," TONED GELATIN SILVER PRINT, 1998, 20 × 24 INCHES (50.8 × 61 CM)

The Soil pieces are the opposite of the Sugar children series. Here, the potting soil is dispersed over a lightbox and then systematically cleaned with the aid of miniature vacuum cleaners, straws, moistened cotton swabs, and other improvised tools. Muniz's interest was to experience drawing on a luminous surface rather than an illuminated one, and to try connecting this concept with that of the photographic negative.

"Binoculars," toned gelatin silver print, 1997, 20 × 24 inches (50.8 × 61 cm)

"Hands," toned gelatin silver print, 1998, 20 × 24 inches (50.8 × 61 cm)

"Fossil," toned gelatin silver print, 1998, 20 × 24 inches (50.8 × 61 cm)

"Snake," toned gelatin silver print, 1999, 20 × 24 inches (50.8 × 61 cm)

"INDIVIDUALS," CIBACHROME PRINT, 1998, 60 × 48 INCHES (152.4 × 122 CM)

"Alfred Hitchcock used Bosco chocolate syrup for the famous shower scene in *Psycho*. Apparently, real blood does not look bloody enough on the screen. There is a major difference between the 'real' and the 'unrealistic,' and sometimes the real thing does not produce a persuasive representation of itself. I chose to work with chocolate because it had something to do with the feeling of painting. Chocolate inspires a multitude of psychological phenomena: it has to do with scatology, desire, sex, addiction, luxury, romance, etc. I have never met anyone who doesn't like chocolate. Freud could probably explain why everybody loves chocolate. That's why he was my first subject. I also wanted to make a drawing that challenged me in time: It usually takes an hour before the chocolate starts to dry and only a few minutes for it to melt under the hot lamps. I have to run a lot, and the studio can get messy."

"Sigmund," cibachrome print, 1997,
60 × 48 inches (152.4 × 122 cm)

Sigmund Freud in chocolate syrup.

"Brando, After Andy Warhol,"
cibachrome print, 1999, 60 × 48 inches
(152.4 × 122 cm)

Actor Marlon Brando in chocolate syrup.

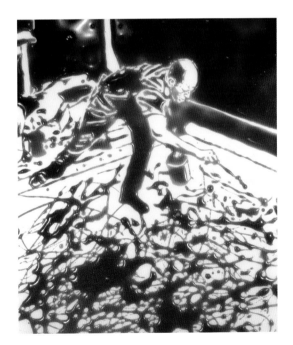

"Action photo, After Hans Namuth," cibachrome print, 1997, 60 x 48 inches (152.4 x 122 cm)

This is a chocolate syrup portrait of artist Jackson Pollack in the middle of creating his action drip painting, inspired by the familiar Hans Namuth photo.

"Burgos Cathedral," cibachrome print, 2003, 60 × 48 inches (152.5 × 122 cm)

"Cathedral of Leon," cibachrome print, 2003, 60 × 48 inches (152.5 × 122 cm)

"DONALD JUDD, 'UNTITLED,' 1965, BARNETT NEWMAN, 'HERE III,' 1965-66, AND CARL ANDRE, 'TWENTY-NINTH COPPER CARDINAL,' 1975, INSTALLED JULY 14-SEPTEMBER 5, 1982, AT THE WHITNEY MUSEUM IN 'SCULPTURE FROM THE PERMANENT COLLECTION,'" SILVER DYE BLEACH PRINT, 2000, 64 × 51 INCHES (162.5 × 129.5 CM)

In 2000, Muniz created a series of nine large-scale photographs based on iconic minimalist and post-minimalist artworks that had been featured in the Whitney Museum in New York. Muniz selected works from the Whitney's collections that were prime examples of the minimalist art movement using materials that first got very real and then began to fall apart. Muniz reasoned that, if Minimalism stripped art down, reducing it to bare, self-referential elements, why couldn't minimalism itself be pared down in the same way?

To create his series, Muniz collected dust from the floors of the museum. He would later state in an interview, "Dust was the hardest substance I've ever worked with, because it's disgusting. Dust is pieces of hair and skin. I think people scratch their heads a lot in museums; that gets mixed in with the residue from the artworks themselves. That's the ultimate bind between the museum visitors and the artwork. If you do a DNA profiling of the material I used, you would end up with a great mailing list." After Muniz recreated the works out of dust, he photographed the drawings and enlarged them; the results were reproductions of reproductions, several times removed from the real thing. The pictures are quite dramatic in their bleakness, more than simple black-and-white photographs of sculptural installations.

"Ad Reinhardt," silver dye bleach print, 2000, 44 × 66 inches (111.5 × 167.5 cm)

"THE GOTHIC ARCH, AFTER PIRANESI," CIBACHROME PRINT, 2002, 100 × 72 INCHES (254 × 183 CM)

Muniz here recreates from memory the work of the 18th century etchings of Giovanni Piranesi's famous Imaginary Prison series, which displays a kind of impossible architecture and strange perspective. Each image took about a month to finish, and is composed entirely out of strings, pins, and shadows, which were re-inscribed into photographs.

"The Drawbridge, After Piranesi," cibachrome print, 2002, $39^{1}/_{2} \times 28^{1}/_{4}$ inches (100×72 cm)

"The Smoking Fire, After Piranesi," cibachrome print, 2002, $39^{1}/_{2} \times 28^{1}/_{4}$ inches (100×72 cm)

"Toy Soldier," cibachrome print, 2003, 92 × 72 inches (233.7 × 182.9 cm)

"I would like people to walk toward a picture, to see how it changes as they walk. Pictures mean different things at different distances. There are always micronarratives being played." Here the soldier is constructed entirely out of plastic war toys.

"Self-Portrait, I'm Too Sad to Tell You, After Bas Jan Ader," cibachrome print, 2003, 72 × 92 inches (182.9 × 233.7 cm)

"MEDUSA MARINARA," CIBACHROME PRINT, 1998, 30-INCH DIAMETER (76.2 CM)

The head of Medusa made out of marinara sauce.

CHAPTER 14

Octavio Ocampo

(1943–)

METAMORPHIC ART

AMBIGUOUS IMAGES, WHICH SEEM to flip-flop in meaning, have been popular for well over a hundred years, and there are even examples that date back several hundred years. Most of the traditional types of ambiguous images involve reversal of the figure/ground relationship, but there is also a different variety, which is not so reliant on figure/ground reversal. In the latter, the contours of the figure are deliberately made ambiguous, and one's perception of it reverses based on how the eye groups those contours into meaningful relationships. It is difficult to perceive both possibilities simultaneously.

Mexican artist Octavio Ocampo has specialized in creating portraits and religious scenes that perceptually "flip-flop." The longer one looks at his work, the more content is revealed: Flowers become faces, mountains speak to each other, and mourners over a coffin become the face of Christ. A devout Catholic, Ocampo imbues his works with religious and secular symbolism.

Ocampo lives in Tepoztlan, a mountainous region southwest of Mexico City. He was born in Celaya, Guanajuato, Mexico in 1943 and started studying art an early age under the influence of his parents, who were in the design business. In the local art school he attended as a young man, Ocampo constructed "papier-mâché" figures for floats, and ornaments that were used during carnival parades and other festivals. It was here that he learned firsthand about art composition, materials, and techniques. In high school, Ocampo painted murals for the preparatory school and the city hall of Celaya. Ruth Rivera (daughter of famed Mexican artist and muralist Diego Rivera) and Maria Luisa "La China" Mendoza saw his work and encouraged him to attend the School of Painting and Sculpture at the National Institute of Fine Arts.

His talents were not limited to painting and sculpture, but extended to acting and dancing as well. While at the San Francisco Art Institute, he studied all these disciplines and pursued both a film and theater career, graduating in 1974. In 1976, he began to devote himself solely to painting and sculpture. He now works primarily in what he calls a "metamorphic style," using a technique of superimposing and juxtaposing realistic and figurative details within the images that he creates. He explained how it evolved: "When I was looking for a definition of a specific style in my work, I did some experimenting. I realized that the metamorphic elements were emerging more frequently in my compositions, so I adopted it as something wonderful—important enough to be regarded as a serious matter in the art fields." Ocampo finds his metamorphic inspiration everywhere: in clouds, trees, water, people, movies, books, photographs, and more. "I may find my resolution awake or sleeping," he said. "Once it is completed in my mind, only the technical aspect remains, that of transferring the idea to materials."

Ocampo states that he lures the viewer in with an intial impression of, say, beauty or horror. But that's just the first image. "Then they realize there is a second image, then a third, and often these carry a different emotional message altogether from the first image."

OCTAVIO OCAMPO AT WORK

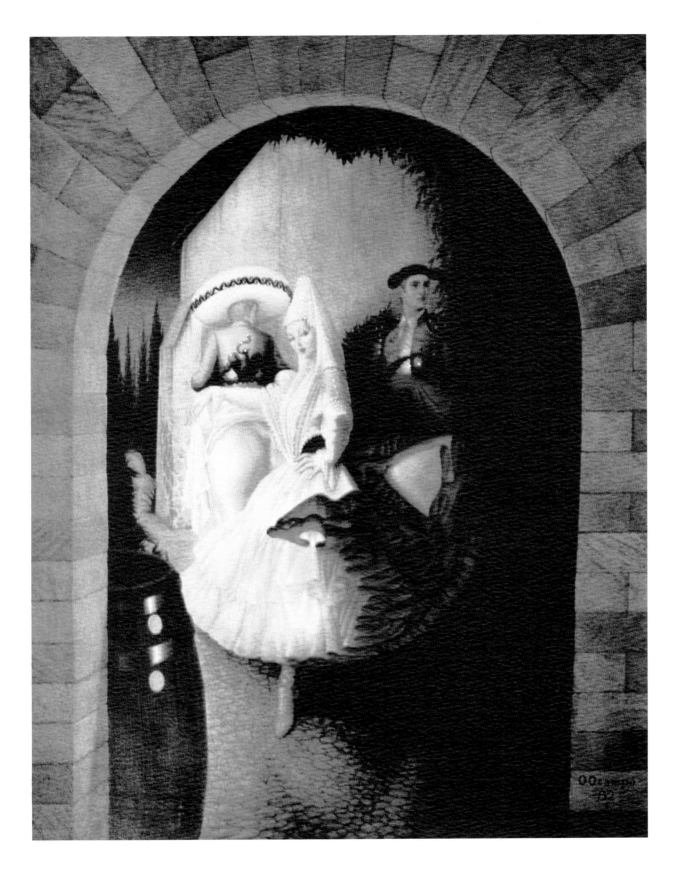

"LUPE," OIL ON CANVAS, 1982

The life of the tragic and tempestuous 1930s Mexican film star Lupe Velez is portrayed.

"Hollywood Lights," oil on canvas, 1982

Hollywood screen idol James Dean is captured in this portrait.

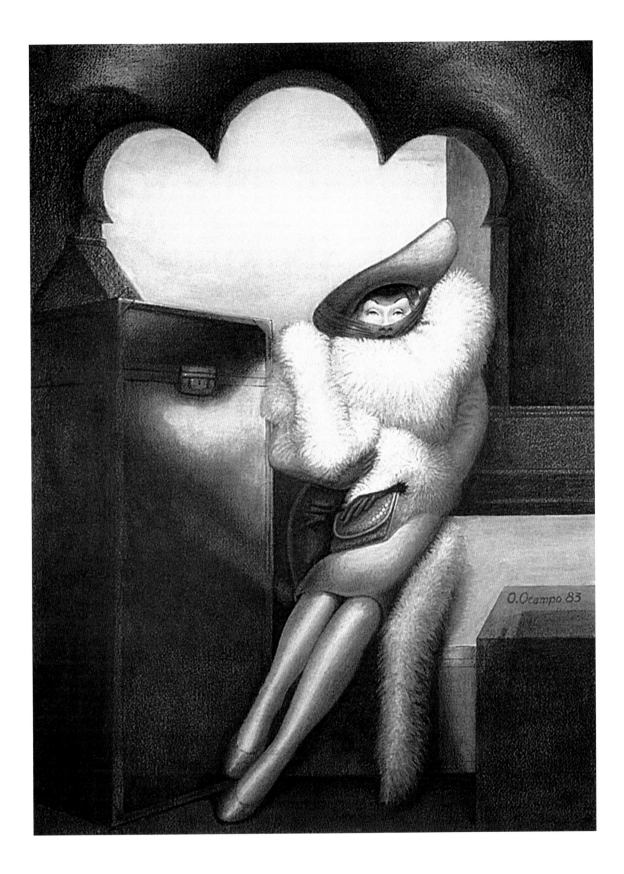

"MARLENE," OIL ON CANVAS, 1983

Ocampo's portrait of 1940s film star Marlene Dietrich is a mastery of ambiguous imagery. The details of her fur coat, trademark hat, and purse blend beautifully into her face.

"FOREVER ALWAYS," OIL ON CANVAS, 1989

In this image, Ocampo depicts a life well lived or one that will be well lived. Those who see the older couple note that they share the Cup of Life (center of the picture) and the crown of fidelity (above the cup). Both of these are symbols of the life they have shared together and the love that fills the cup with a golden light.

The older couple sees each other as they were when they were much younger, when they courted with serenades while drinking tequila with limes (lower center). The viewer is able to look into the older man's mind to note that he always sees his chosen as beautiful and desirable. Those who view the younger couple see that they are looking forward to sharing a cup full of love and happiness. This commitment becomes their crowning achievement, symbolized by the ring (crown) they wear. The young man remembers how his love came out of her house in response to his serenades.

"VISIONS OF QUIXOTE," OIL ON CANVAS, 1989

In this image, Ocampo tells the story of Don Quixote by the use of a single picture.

From afar, the viewer sees an old man with a faraway and dreamlike expression on his face. Wild yellow hair and a strange beard serve to complete the man's odd demeanor. Drawing closer, the viewer is transported to the Spanish countryside, where one notices that the windmills in the center of the picture look like they are about to come to life.

Two proud heroes occupy the center of the picture and are backed by windmills: Don Quixote on his faithful steed Rocinante and Sancho Panza on Dappie. They are surrounded by the world that lives in Don Quixote's mind.

In the middle of the right picture, Don Quixote is immortalized, crying out in protest that a deceased man still lives, and readying himself to hijack his body to save him from an untimely funeral. If you focus on the area around this scene, you will see the face of a dog—a symbol of Quixote's madness.

The middle left of the picture shows Xarifa working in the fields. Again this scene appears to be the face of a dog, to show the madness of imagining her to be Dulcinea (pictured in the upper left-hand corner). Above Xarifa in the fields, the village of La Mancha is pictured surrounded by mythical dragons and sea monsters.

Above the village, sits the Duke's castle (upper left) with the Duke's face pictured in the castle's wall. Careful observation will reveal a skull outlining the left side of the castle, a hint of the Duke's sinister plans for our heroes. The upper right side of the painting shows Miguel de Cervantes' ghostly face watching over his work. While the hills, rocks, and dates alter with the power of the Man of La Mancha's madness.

"CELESTIAL BODIES," OIL ON CANVAS, 1994

Angels comprise both the head and the hands.

"Mona Lisa's Chair," oil on canvas, 1988

The picture consists of a chair occupied by three rabbits, one black (on the lower left) and two whites (in the lower center). A cat sits on the chair's upper cushions (middle center) and watches the viewer of the piece. The chair has a mirrored back, that at first glance appears to be the face of Mona Lisa, but upon closer inspection actually consists of two women, a man, an angel, as well as a skyline. The background in "Mona Lisa's Chair" is a study of the subconscious mind as face turns into forms and nothing is really what it seems at first.

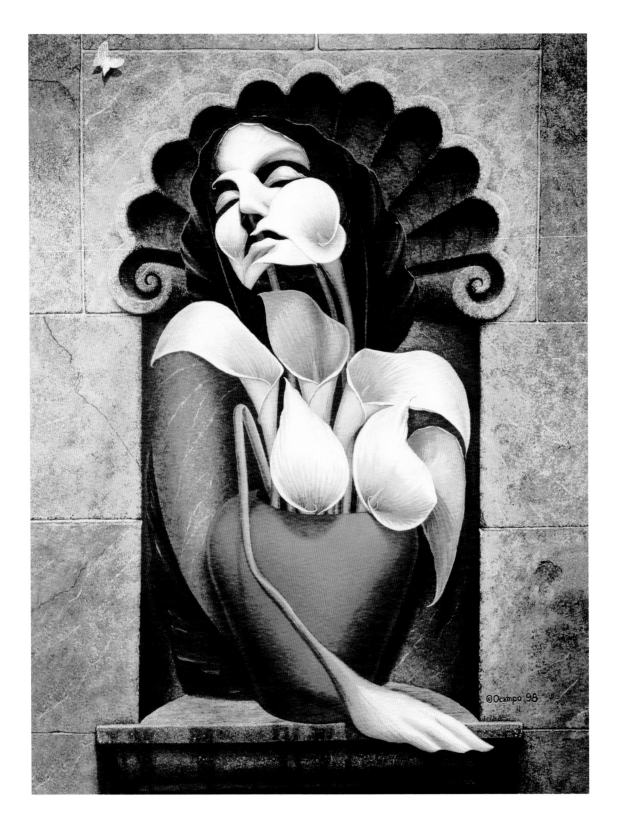

"ECSTASY OF THE LILIES," OIL ON CANVAS, 1998

Ocampo's "Ecstasy of the Lilies," depicts a girl dressed up for her "Coming out Party," which is symbolic of her official transition from girlhood to womanhood, where she experiences the power, passion, and energy that is the threshold of awakening. The lilies are indoors, alluding to her eventual role as the heart and soul of the "home." The artist keeps her innocence intact through this transition by keeping her eyes closed to the world.

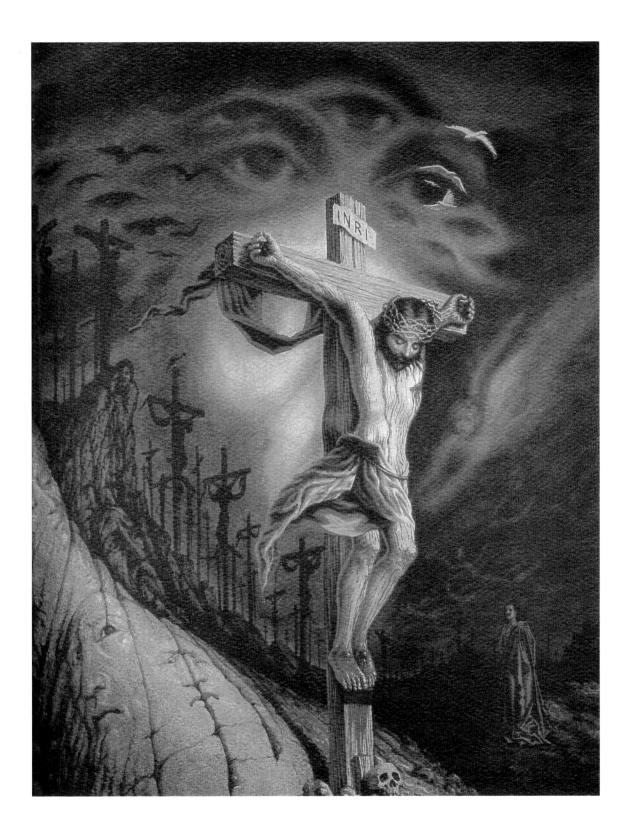

"Calvary," oil on canvas, undated

"Calvary" is Ocampo's religious painting of hope, and is filled with sacred symbolism. Christ's face is heavy with sorrow as he is crucified on the Cross. Through the face of Jesus' suffering, we can see the crucifixion that, according to the Bible, is the sacrifice Christ made for all humanity. The middle left side of the painting depicts the sacrifices later made by Christian martyrs.

"Palm Sunday," oil on canvas, 1994

In his vision of Palm Sunday, Octavio Ocampo depicts Christ's entry into Jerusalem.

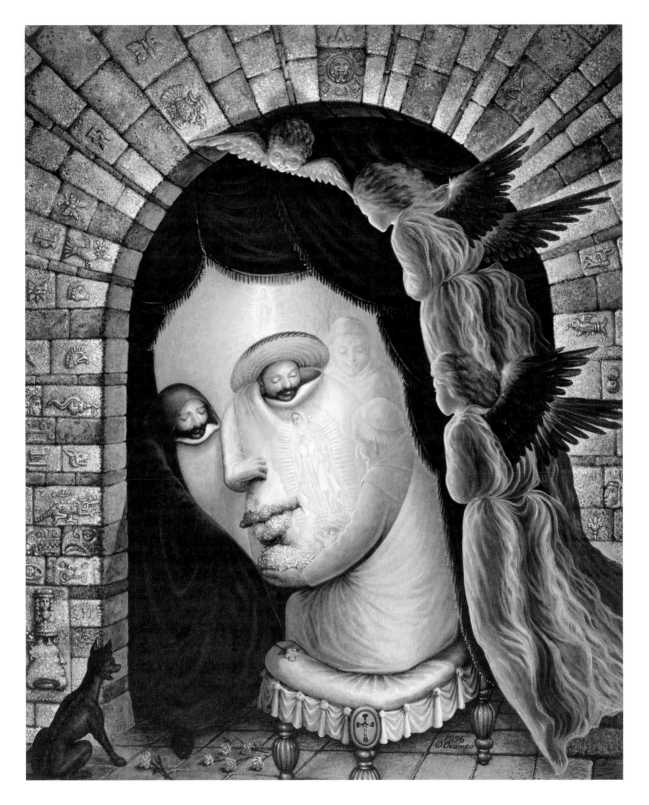

"Miracle of the Roses" is a depiction of the culmination of the story of Our Lady of Guadeloupe, the Virgin Mary. Pictured in this painting is the culminating scene of the story where Juan Diego comes into the Bishop's presence bearing the proof from the Virgin. He lets go of his tabard showering the astonished Bishop with roses, only to find that the symbol of the Madonna is now indelibly marked on the front of his tabard. His tabard can still be seen in the cathedral that was built to honor the Virgin.

CHAPTER 15

István Orosz

(1951–)

ANAMORPHOSES

"István Orosz is in many ways Escher's artistic heir—a master of graphic technique, a keen observer with a sly wit, a conjurer who can make the impossible believable, an artist who can harness difficult visual and mathematical tools to achieve breathtakingly clever effects."
—DORIS SCHATTSCHNEIDER

"The mysterious world of illusions in Orosz's pictures draws you into a perfect world, the irrational construction of which is hidden behind the aesthetics of the imagination and the lyricism of forgotten beauty."
—MARTA SYLVESTROVA

HUNGARIAN ARTIST ISTVÁN OROSZ is a master of the anamorphic technique. He is incredibly adept at hiding portraits and other objects within a scene. Growing up under Communist rule, Orosz became quite familiar with the art of crafting images with hidden meanings. Throughout his career, Orosz has always been drawn to tricks of perspective and optical illusions, and incorporated many illusionistic concepts into his graphic posters. At a 1996 international graphic design symposium, he stated,

Advertising and publicity try to show the things better and more desirable than they actually are, so people are beguiled. A majority agrees that this is the task of advertising because it is needed for business. The ethical problems are often overlooked. This question looks even greater in the case of works that use optical illusions and paradoxes. Or does not? Maybe these visual tricks just call attention to the "whopping lies."

In his spectacularly executed engravings, Orosz has explored ambiguous imagery, impossible figures, inverted figures, and anamorphoses, which he brings to life in works that display his admiration for classical antiquity. In many of his nonanamorphic illusionistic prints, you can see conceptual inspiration from the illusionistic works of Shigeo Fukuda, Giuseppe Arcimboldo, M.C. Escher, Sandro Del Prete, Roger Shepard, Salvador Dalí, and René Magritte.

Orosz frequently uses the pseudonym ΟΨΤΙΣ, which in Greek means "nobody." Orosz explains the use of his pseudonym:

> When years ago Andras Torok gave me this pseudonym, I obviously did not have a clue how relevant my new name would turn out to be. Before me was the most cunning of all Homer's heroes, Odysseus, who was given this name in his fight against the Cyclops. As we all know, the Cyclops lost his sight in this battle. Much of my work at that time fell into the domain of *trompe l'oeil*. The person who gave me this name must have thought that *trompe l'oeil* was also an

A STRETCHED SELF-PORTRAIT, 2001

Odysseus-ΟΨΤΙΣ, attitude. It represented an attack against the eye, more gentle certainly than that of crafty Odysseus, being nothing more than a trick of the eye.

István Orosz was born in Kecskemét, Hungary in 1951. He was trained as a graphic designer, not in painting proper, at the Budapest Academy of Applied Arts. He also learned animated film techniques at Pannonia Film Studios. Stage design for various theaters in Hungary was his first area of professional practice. Later, when the poster became his prime avocation, he created them for theaters and movies, and during the pro-democratic movement in Hungary, political posters as well. His progressive political posters brought him great acclaim and international recognition.

Additional works and an interview with Orosz can be seen at http://neuro.caltech.edu/~seckel/mod/.

OROSZ ISTVÁN
GRAFIKUSMŰVÉSZ
KIÁLLÍTÁSA
FERENCVÁROSI
PINCETÁRLAT
1979. III. 29-IV. 10.

A self-reflective pun: An image of Orosz hanging up a poster for his own poster exhibition in Budapest, 1979

This is considered by many to be Orosz's masterpiece of hidden anamorphosis, and it was his first attempt at using this technique to conceal a portrait. It depicts a shipwreck scene in the frozen North based on the novel "The Mysterious Island" by the famous 19th century French science-fiction author Jules Verne. The portrait is visible only when you look at the reflection on the cylinder when the latter is placed over the moon. A movie of this anamorphosis is on the website http://neuro.caltech.edu/~seckel/mod/.

"HOMER ON THE BEACH," ETCHING, 1996, $34^3/4 \times 18$ INCHES (88.4×45.7 CM)

The bust of Homer is seen on the reflecting cylinder.

"THE WELL," ETCHING, 1998, 23 × 18 INCHES (58.4 × 45.7 CM)

DETAIL FROM "THE WELL"

This hidden anamorphic portrait in homage to M. C. Escher is based on a pictorial challenge originally given to Escher by his friend Bruno Ernst, but left unresolved because of Escher's rapidly failing health. The challenge was to create a scene in which a mirror was placed to show the surrounding areas otherwise hidden from view. With the encouragement of Ernst, Orosz took up the problem and, imagining himself in the mind of Escher, explored some ways in which Escher may have approached it.

The print depicts the church at Atrani, visible only in a mirror strategically placed in a tangled garden with a break in its wall. However, Orosz went far beyond the original problem by creating the extra surprise of a hidden portrait of Escher that is revealed when placed over the well. The use of a curved mirror to portray Escher is particularly appropriate, as Escher used a spherical mirror in some of his best-known prints, most notably his 1925 self-portrait, "Hand With Reflecting Sphere." A movie of "The Well" is on the website http://neuro.caltech.edu/~seckel/mod/.

"SELF-PORTRAIT WITH EINSTEIN," AQUARELLE COLORED PEN AND INK DRAWING, 2002,
23$^1/_2$ × 31$^1/_2$ INCHES (60 × 80 CM)

A portrait of Albert Einstein, which is revealed when placed on the image of a mirror in the center. There is much in the sense of play in this drawing, as Orosz's own face can be seen reflected in the mirror that is drawn on the image.

"Dionysius Theater," etching, 1986, $15^{1}/_{2} \times 23^{1}/_{2}$ inches (40 × 60 cm)

Two travelers come across the ruins of an ancient Greek theater. When the reflective cylinder is appropriately placed in the center of the abandoned stage, the head of the Minotaur can be seen.

"LABYRINTH OF THESEUS," ETCHING WITH REFLECTIVE PYRAMID, 1986, 19$^1/_2$ × 27$^1/_2$ INCHES (50 × 70 CM)

Theseus is revealed in the reflective pyramid.

"LABYRINTH OF THE MINOTAUR," ETCHING
WITH REFLECTIVE CONE, 1986,
19$^1/_2$ × 27$^1/_2$ INCHES (50 × 70 CM)

This is the first of a series of labyrinth anamorphoses devoted to the ancient Greek legend of the hero Theseus and his battle with the Minotaur, a powerful creature with a human body and the head of a bull, in a labyrinth designed by the legendary artificer Daedalus. This prison was created to contain the monster—a place from which none could return unless they knew the secret way through its tortuous passageways. Theseus extracted the secret of the passageways from Minos' daughter Ariadne, who fell in love with him. Theseus used a ball of thread and unwound it as he entered so that he could retrace his steps. Theseus killed the Minotaur, emerged from the labyrinth, and immediately set sail for Athens with Ariadne and his fellow sailors.

"ATLANTIS I," ETCHING WITH CYLINDER, 1999,
$27^1/_2 \times 27^1/_2$ INCHES (70 × 70 CM)

"ATLANTIS II," ETCHING WITH INVERTED HANGING
CONE, 1999, $27^1/_2 \times 27^1/_2$ INCHES (70 × 70 CM)

"ATLANTIS III," ETCHING WITH FIVE-SIDED PYRAMID, 1999, $27^1/_2 \times 27^1/_2$ INCHES (70 × 70 CM)

These three anamorphoses that depict the sinking of the lost continent of Atlantis, use differently configured reflecting anamorphoscopes to represent the ocean overtaking the famed land.

"SELF-PORTRAIT OF ESCHER IN AN ANAMORPHIC CYLINDER," ETCHING WITH REFLECTIVE CYLINDER, 1998,
$11^1/_2 \times 15^1/_4$ INCHES (29 × 39 CM), $5^1/_2 \times 2^1/_4$ INCHES (14 × 6 CM)

This anamorphic portrait was created for the Escher Centenary Congress celebrations held in Italy in 1998. It is based on one that Escher created himself. A movie of this anamorphosis is on the website http://neuro.caltech.edu/~seckel/mod/.

"ANAMORPHIC BODY LANDSCAPES I, II, III, IV," PENCIL DRAWINGS, 1989, $23^{1}/_{2} \times 23^{1}/_{2}$ INCHES (60 × 60 CM)

"Anna in Seaside," acrylic on canvas with reflective cylinder, 2001,
55 × 39 1/2 × 39 1/2 inches (140 × 100 × 100 cm)

Orosz was inspired to do this oblique anamorphosis of Shakespeare after reading a short passage from Shakespeare's Richard II:

> For sorrow's eye, glazed with blinding tears,
> Divides one thing entire to many objects;
> Like perspectives, which rightly gaz'd upon
> Show nothing but confusion, ey'd awry
> Distinguish form.

The word "perspective" had wider meaning at that time, and referred to every strange and new method for opening up spaces, and to all anamorphic pictures, i.e., those that change their meaning if seen from another viewpoint or distance. Orosz's self-portrait can be seen at the bottom of the top image.

"THE MIRROR," ETCHING, 1998, $38^{1}/_{4} \times 26^{3}/_{4}$ INCHES (97.2 × 68.3 CM)

In this work, Orosz plays with the ambiguity of depth and mirrors. Which is the real reflection, and which is not? Also, note that the cubes on the floor are ambiguous in depth.

"Portrait of Shakespeare," Poster Print, 1999, $39^{1}/_{4} \times 14^{1}/_{2}$ inches (100 × 37 cm)

The use of the two theatrical musicians to create Shakespeare's face says much about Shakespeare as a creature of the theater. This poster won first prize at a graphic-design poster competition held at the Victoria and Albert Museum in London.

"Mysterious Island," Poster Print, 1979, 19^1/$_2$ × 27^1/$_2$ inches (50 × 70 cm)

A portrait of Jules Verne is seen in this topsy-turvy illustration, which would later become the basis of Orosz's well-known anamorphic hidden portrait of Jules Verne and the Mysterious Island.

"Escher in Italy," etching, 1987, $19^{1}/_{2} \times 13^{1}/_{2}$ inches (50 × 34.5 cm)

A picture of M. C. Escher is hidden in this scene. Escher spent a great deal of time in Italy.

CHAPTER 16

John Pugh

(1957–)

TROMPE L'OEIL

"*The Webster's dictionary definition of* monumental *most suitably describes the murals of John Pugh. They are massive and imposing, exceptionally great in both conception and execution, and are most assuredly of historical and enduring significance.*"

—KEVIN BRUCE

"*It seems almost universal that people take delight in being visually tricked. Once captivated by the illusion, the viewer is lured to cross an artistic threshold and thus seduced into exploring the concept of the piece. I have also found that by creating an architectural illusion that integrates with the existing environment, both optically and aesthetically, the art transcends the 'separateness' that public art sometimes produces.*"

—JOHN PUGH

JOHN PUGH'S *TROMPE L'OEIL* MURALS are so lifelike that they cause mishaps and confusion for the unsuspecting. In 1981, after the completion of his first major project, the mural in Taylor Hall on the California State University, Chico campus, several fender benders occurred because motorists were distracted by what looks like a gaping hole in the building.

Because his art is so realistic, people often take it for photorealism, which Pugh says it is not. "I'm not projecting a photo up on the wall and painting it," he explains. "What I do is a little different than that—a little more original. Illusion has a universal appeal; everyone likes being tricked. Once captivated, the viewer is then invited into the concept and thus begins the journey. Providing this experience is demonstrative of human interest in a pure form."

Pugh is passionate about *trompe l'oeil* being used as a fine art form. While he considers light, color, and perspective intrinsic to the craft, it is the context that Pugh says lifts *trompe l'oeil* into the realm of fine art. Something must be imparted other than an illusion, Pugh believes, a value beyond mystery or mere decoration. He states,

> I have found that the "language" of life-sized illusions allows me to communicate with a very large audience. It is important for me, as an artist, to interact with the community, formulating concepts based upon a multitude of viewpoints. Artists must be continually aware that their work can serve as a bridge between diverse cultural backgrounds. Public art is of great interest to me, providing me with a sense of purpose, as it is a very powerful form of communication. It can link people together, stimulate a sense of pride within the community, and introduce the viewer to new ideas and perspectives.

Most of the time Pugh responds to existing architectural settings. He has also had the opportunity to take part in the development of the architecture itself, modifying the design of the structure to marry his painting to the site. This bridge between the art and the architecture can effectively erase the transition point between reality and illusion. In this way his art becomes integrated into the real world of architecture and lends credibility to the illusion of the painting. Together the whole is greater than the sum of its parts. He writes,

> When developing a mural, I also respond to aspects of the location such as its architectural style or the natural surroundings. Often, I like to play with the art's context by contrasting these environments with another place and/or time. This paradox or juxtaposition of environments transports the viewer on a journey from local reality into a new space. During this "voyage," the viewer may experience sequential discoveries as my compositions are designed to unfold in narrative layers.

John Pugh was born in Illinois in 1957 and moved to Northern California when he was a child. His art-loving parents encouraged his creative interests and talent at an early age. "All kids start doing artistic things in kindergarten," Pugh commented in a recent magazine interview; "I did too, only I never let it die." It was at the California State University in the town of Chico (a small agricultural and educational center several hours northeast of San Francisco) that Pugh decided on a career using his natural talent and love for art. After taking a semester's leave to work as a carpenter, he resumed his art studies with renewed dedication. Based on the success of several small murals he had created during the previous three years, he was rewarded with his first major commission, a *trompe l'oeil* mural on a wall of Taylor Hall, which housed, among other liberal arts disciplines, the Chico State Art Department. Begun in the fall of 1980 and completed in the spring of 1981, this mural would receive international recognition and launch Pugh's career in a spectacular fashion. Twenty years later, his alma mater would award him its Distinguished Alumnus Award.

Since 1978, Pugh has completed over 200 murals. He lives in Truckee, California, with his wife Wendy. He has a studio in the Santa Cruz mountains where several apprentices and associates work with him.

Additional works and interviews with John Pugh can be found on the website http://neuro.caltech.edu/~seckel/mod/.

PUGH AT WORK DESIGNING HIS NEXT MURAL, 2002

PUGH AT WORK, 2002

"TAYLOR HALL," ACRYLIC ON STUCCO, 1981, 24 × 36 FEET (7.3 × 11 METERS)

Taylor Hall is a local landmark at the California State University located in Chico. Pugh's mural has received international attention, because so many people have been bewildered by what they saw as they went past; in fact, the mural has caused a number of fender benders.

Pugh reminisces about his painting on Taylor Hall: "I kept eyeing that particular wall. It has a northeastern exposure with little sun, a smooth surface, and it is perpendicular to traffic—better for a perspective illusion. Plus, it is the downtown entrance to the university with a lot of pedestrian traffic."

Pugh's idea for the mural was inspired by a dream he had in which he witnessed the wall "breaking open." He also considered what people passing that corner might imagine was inside Taylor Hall. "I liked the idea of visually excavating the building to expose a particular imagined vision," he says. "The modern educational façade is broken away to reveal the ancient Greek academe—the essence of our educational system."

"Siete Punto Uno," acrylic on M.D.O. board, 1990, 16 × 24 feet (4.9 × 7.3 meters)

In 1989, the town of Los Gatos, California, suffered significant damage from an earthquake that measured 7.1 on the Richter scale. The mural, "Siete Punto Uno" (Spanish for "7.1"), is located on the outside of Pasteria restaurant on Main Street in downtown Los Gatos. Considered the propitiator of earthquakes, the Mayan jaguar god (as represented in the mural) is grafted with the "cats" of Los Gatos, becoming one of the image's key metaphors.

The woman standing in the street and looking into the room is also painted.

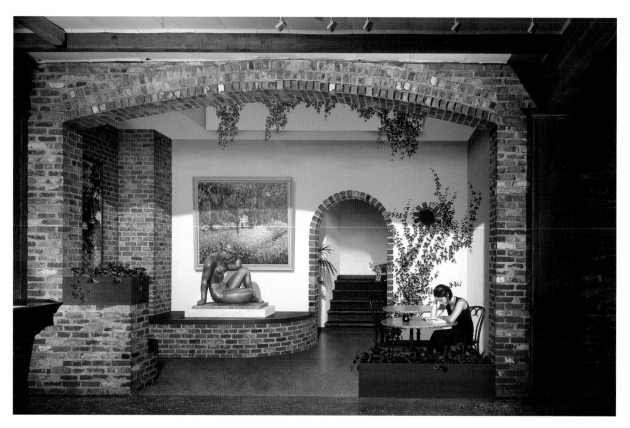

"ART IMITATING LIFE IMITATING ART IMITATING LIFE," ACRYLIC ON M.D.O. BOARD, 1996,
13 × 19^1/$_2$ FEET (4 × 6 METERS)

At a café in San Jose, California, which features this mural by Pugh, a customer complained he had received the "silent treatment" when he tried to introduce himself to the pretty woman reading a book.

CLOSE-UP DETAIL OF THE PAINTED
SCULPTURE AND PAINTING

PUGH PAINTS THE STATUE FEATURED IN "ART IMITATING LIFE"

"Joshua Tree Chronicles," acrylic on M.D.O. board, 1998, 5 × 18 feet (1.5 × 5.5 meters)

First-time visitors to the mural at Victor Valley College Library in Victorville, California, are convinced that the canvas is unraveling and that the wooden stretcher bars are three-dimensional. Intrigued after realizing the entire surface is flat (including the hanging canvas shape), they bond with and explore the piece further by "uncovering" its layers. The mural is a tribute to the history of Victor Valley and contains three layers symbolizing distinct subjects and eras; including petroglyphs left from Piute indians.

"SILENT STREAM," ACRYLIC ON CANVAS, 1999, 8 × 14 FEET (2.4 × 4.3 METERS)

This mural was conceived to comfort and inspire, and can be found in the main lobby of the Kaiser Permanente Hospital in Santa Clara, California. The mural invites the viewer to set adrift in a meditative water garden. The Hepworth-like bronze and marble sculpture—reminiscent of a seashell with a blue pearl—serves as a sacred centerpiece. The harp strings seem to echo a distant melody like an ancient song of the sea.

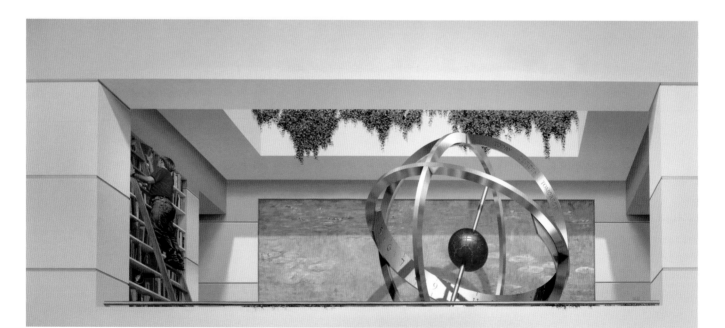

"STUDY WITH SPHERE AND WATER," ACRYLIC ON NON-WOVEN MEDIA, 1999, 12 × 29³/₄ FEET (3.7 × 9.1 METERS)

This mural, located in the University Center of the University of Florida, Jacksonville, depicts a meditative space of learning and inspiration.

"VALENTINE'S DAY," ACRYLIC ON STUCCO, 2000, 49³/₄ × 15 FEET (15.2 × 4.6 METERS)

This mural is located in Twentynine Palms, California. Obviously, the historical theme of "Cattle Days in Hidden Valley" is not the only subject of this mural. It also depicts an artist falling asleep while finishing the mural. Of course, the artist, his scaffolding, the buzzard, and the cow standing nearby are all painted illusions.

The subtle two-dimensional qualities of the "unfinished" mural provide a contrast with the foreground and heighten the sense of illusion. If the background were less complete, there would not be enough colors or shapes for a full composition. If it were more complete, it would be a distraction and render the illusion less effective. This work also provides the viewer with a journey through all the different steps of mural painting—from wall grids and sketched images to blocked-in colors and finished painting.

"Woman in Café," acrylic on canvas, 2000, 6 × 5 feet (1.82 × 1.52 meters)

This is Pugh's homage to Edouard Manet's famous painting "Le Bar aux Folies-Bergère." "I tweaked [the painting] by superimposing a contemporary woman in front of the woman who is normally in the painting," says Pugh, "so it's shifting time within the piece and playing off a classic piece"—a technique that artists have used for centuries.

"LIGHT WALK," ACRYLIC ON NON-WOVEN MEDIA (LEFT PORTION), 2001, 6 × 26 FEET (1.82 × 7.92 METERS)

"LIGHT WALK," ACRYLIC ON NON-WOVEN MEDIA (RIGHT PORTION), 2001, 6 × 26 FEET (1.82 × 7.92 METERS)

This mural, located in the patient area of the oncology department in the Palo Alto Medical Foundation in northern California, was designed to create a healing and reflective environment. The viewer is invited on a dreamquest into this exotic underworld—a spiritual path with reflecting pools, sacred sculptures, and bridges that lead up into the treetops. Before the moss wall stands a young woman made of bronze, in sublime rapture. On the left, as an homage to Rodin's sculpture of Victor Hugo, is a prophet of white marble.

DETAIL OF "LIGHT WALK"

"Bath of Venus," acrylic on canvas, 2002, $5^{1}/_{2} \times 9^{1}/_{4}$ feet (1.7×2.8 meters)

Everything in this image is painted, including the bowl, ledge, and wine glass. Art patrons at the show where this painting was displayed actually spilled their wine trying to set their own goblets on the "ledge."

"THE DIRT ON BISHOP," ACRYLIC ON M.D.O. BOARD, 2002,
10 × 10 FEET (3 × 3 METERS)

DETAIL OF "THE DIRT ON BISHOP"

This mural, located in Bishop, California, represents a sedimentary survey of the town's heritage. Digging down through the bullets, spurs, horseshoes, railroad spikes, rusted water valves, and old keys, we unlock different parts of Bishop's history. Following the Bristlecone pine roots we dig deeper: past Paiute arrowheads and beads, and through fossilized Mammoth tusks and Sabertooth skulls. Delving even deeper we pass fossils of ancient roots, prehistoric leaves, and trilobites to reach layers that date back to the beginning of the world. On the lighter side, a dog named Hunter helps to "ground" this piece as he sniffs the air for a bone from the floor above, but picks up the scent of an eon.

"Reverse, Lateral, and Loop," acrylic on MDO board, 2002, 13 × 70 feet (396 × 2134 cm)

This mural, located in downtown Tehachapi, California, makes reference to two subjects that highlight the colorful history of the town The first, "Reverse and Lateral," refers to the type of faults that caused a 7.4 magnitude earthquake in 1952 that destroyed most of this small downtown. Many lives were lost, and the wall on which this mural is painted was one of the only two structures left standing.

The second subject is the internationally celebrated "Tehachapi Loop." The loop concept was suggested by a nine-year-old water boy when railroad engineers were trying to solve the problem of maintaining a required train grade on the steep Tehachapi ascent. As depicted in the mural, the trains literally circle over themselves as they climb up to the pass.

The interplay of the train and the vertical rift as they bisect each other creates a different kind of pathway shape, and a different way of perceiving the town's heritage.

Detail of "Reverse, Lateral, and Loop."

CHAPTER 17

Oscar Reutersvärd

(1915–2001)

IMPOSSIBLE FIGURES

"Reutersvärd's work is still unbeatable in its substructure, clarity, and economy of expression."
— ZENON KULPA

"I give the phenomenon of absurdity a kind of existence." — OSCAR REUTERSVÄRD

SWEDISH ARTIST OSCAR REUTERSVÄRD is generally considered "the father of impossible figures." Although impossible figures in works of art have appeared sporadically since Roman times, either as mistakes in perspective or as visual jokes, Reutersvärd was the first to see them as new and worthy of a serious subject to explore. His systematic approach to exploring impossible figures could justifiably be called "artistic research." His drawings are the intuitive, sensual, and informal work of an artist, and at the same time a systematic approach of a scientist exploring a new dimension—a world that does not exist, a theoretical world that in our terms can only be called "impossible."

Oscar Reutersvärd was born in Stockholm in 1915. At an early age, he had trouble learning, the result of a severe problem with dyslexia. He also had great difficulty estimating the size and distance of objects.

In his early teenage years, Reutersvärd developed a passion for art. In this regard he was fortunate, because he was greatly encouraged by an artistic family. Reutersvärd's sister was also interested in pursuing an artistic career. Together the family worked at home, painting and creating various sculptures.

In 1934, while doodling in a Latin grammar notebook during class, Reutersvärd formed an impossible triangle from a peculiar arrangement of cubes. As he was elaborating on a six-pointed star with a circle of cubes, he discovered that the cubes had formed a strange and impossible construction. After the class, he showed the drawing to one of his classmates, Jan Cornell, who told him that it appeared quite original. They tried researching the topic at the local library, but they were not able to find any similar examples. However, they regarded the figure as only a curiosity and did not attempt to publish it.

During the mid- to late 1930s, Reutersvärd started experimenting with various impossible designs, which resulted in the creation of the first impossible staircase (1937) and concepts related to the well-known impossible fork. However, at the time these were labeled as nothing more than oddities, and no one took them seriously.

It wasn't until 1958 that his old friend Jan Cornell showed him the now classic article on impossible figures and objects by Lionel and Roger Penrose, which featured their independently created versions of an impossible triangle and staircase. The fact that the article was published by two distinguished scientists in a reputable scientific journal gave a great deal of credence to experimenting with such figures—someone other than Reutersvärd was taking them seriously.

In the years 1961 to 1962, Reutersvärd was introduced to the work of M. C. Escher. Reutersvärd was particularly intrigued by Escher's two prints of impossible buildings—"Waterfall" and "Ascending and Descending," which were directly inspired by the impossible triangle and staircase featured in the Penrose article.

Reutersvärd was particularly intrigued by Escher's "Waterfall." For the first time, he could see that impossible figures were being incorporated into serious works of art. This completely renewed his interest in impossible figures, and he started exploring them in a rigorous fashion. He created other original impossible figures, and in 1963 had a first showing of his work at a distinguished gallery in Stockholm. Unfortunately, local art critics reacted to the new form of drawing with either complete lack of interest or total disdain. As they left the gallery, many people shook their heads in disappointment. For Reutersvärd, this show was a total artistic setback.

Moreover, Reutersvärd did not receive any encouragement from his wife Britt, who was herself a serious abstract artist. She didn't like his drawings either and thought that he was wasting his time on ridiculous things. As it turned out, his wife became his best critic. Every time he showed her a new drawing, and she did not find anything amiss with it, he knew that it was wrong. Conversely, if she found something wrong with the image, then he knew it was correct.

Reutersvärd always preferred to draw with India ink on Japanese rice paper or Swedish linen rags. He never allowed himself to draw with a ruler or to employ any mechanical devices. He preferred to draw freehand, which he did when he went by train from Lund to Stockholm—a ten hour journey. As a result, all the lines in his drawings, which he called "living lines," are a bit shaky. He would explain that the shaking from the train helped give more life to his drawings. Their color came from Japanese colored chalk, but sometimes he preferred not to paint them at all.

In 1963 and 1964, Reutersvärd wrote Escher two letters in which he expressed his great admiration for his work, but Escher did not reply. Reutersvärd also sent him extracts from articles on his work appearing in Swedish newspapers. Once again, Escher failed to respond. The only slight bit of encouragement came from a meeting with the famous surrealist painter Marcel Duchamp in Stockholm. At that time Duchamp had drawn a kind of impossible figure, and encouraged Reutersvärd to publish his own work.

By 1964, Reutersvärd had accepted the fact that his drawings were not going to achieve any recognition, much less provide an income. So he accepted a more prestigious professorship in art history at the Royal University of Lund, where he taught for over seventeen years.

However, in the late 1960s, Reutersvärd began to attract a following and his influence started to grow, especially after some books on impossible figures were published that featured his work. Exhibitions were arranged for him in Paris, London, Holland, Japan, Poland, Switzerland, Italy, and Russia. Books featuring his impossible figures were published in English, Swedish, Russian, Polish, and German.

In 1980 the Swedish government recognized his artistic achievements by commissioning three of his impossible drawings for postage stamps. These stamps were produced in 1982 and issued for about two years, until the Swedish government changed the rate of postage. The remaining unused stamps were subsequently destroyed by the Swedish government; they are now quite scarce and eagerly sought by stamp collectors.

Throughout the 1980s and 1990s, Reutersvärd continued to create literally hundreds of impossible figures. He was particularly fond of creating impossible meanderings and paradoxes within a window. He filled many notebooks with impossible figures, each one a new variation. He also started experimenting with impossible anaglyphs, drawings which, when seen through a pair of blue/red filtered glasses, would suggest the figure in 3-D.

In the mid 1990s, he began to be recognized for his work, some of which was commissioned for public buildings in Sweden. The greatest honor came when his drawings and paintings were prominently displayed in the National Museum as well as in the Modern Museum, both in Stockholm. Even so, what always gave him the greatest joy was introducing children to the paradoxes of impossible figures. It was during this period that he also became interested in designing mazes and constructing metallic sculptures made from chains.

In the late 1990s his health sadly started to decline rapidly, and he passed away in 2001.

Additional works and interviews with Reutersvard can be seen at http://neuro.caltech.edu/~seckel/mod/.

PHOTO OF REUTERSVÄRD BY BRUNO ERNST

REUTERSVÄRD HARD AT WORK FINISHING A PICTURE
FOR HIS 1979 SHOW IN THE GALLERY OF
SAINT PETRI IN LUND, SWEDEN.

SHOWING HIS IMPOSSIBLE FIGURES TO CHILDREN
WAS ONE OF REUTERSVÄRD'S PASSIONS, 1991

ANOTHER WORK FINISHED, 1996

"AFTER OPUS 1," FELT-TIP PEN DRAWING, JAPANESE
RICE PAPER, 1981, 12 × 9 INCHES (30.5 × 23 CM)

This drawing was based on the first impossible figure that
Reutersvärd created in 1934.

"Endless Meanderings," colored felt-tip pen drawing, Japanese rice paper, undated,
12 × 9 inches (30.5 × 23 cm)

"Criss-Cross Paradox," colored felt-tip pen drawing, Japanese rice paper, undated,
12 × 9 inches (30.5 × 23 cm)

perspective japonaise n° 270 ab

"An Impossible Configuration with Three Cubes," colored felt-tip pen drawing, Japanese Rice paper, undated, 12 × 9 inches (30.5 × 23 cm)

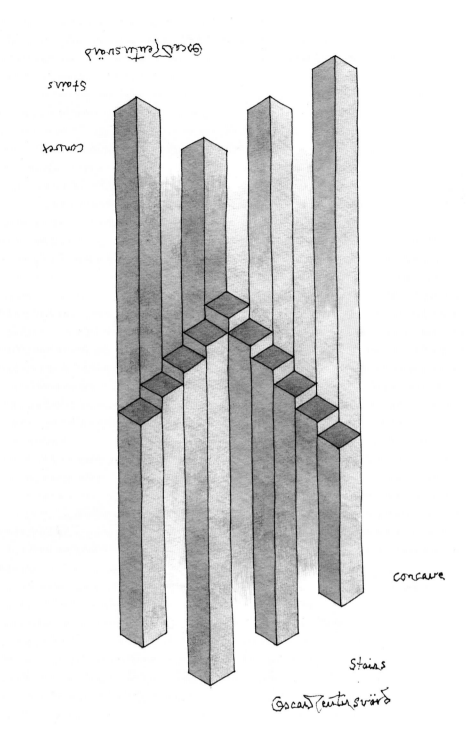

Stairs

concave

Stairs

Oscar Reutersvärd

**"TOPSY-TURVY PARADOX," COLORED FELT-TIP PEN DRAWING, JAPANESE RICE PAPER, UNDATED,
12 × 9 INCHES (30.5 × 23 CM)**

This is one of the few known topsy-turvy impossible figures. In one orientation the stairs are concave, while in another they are convex.

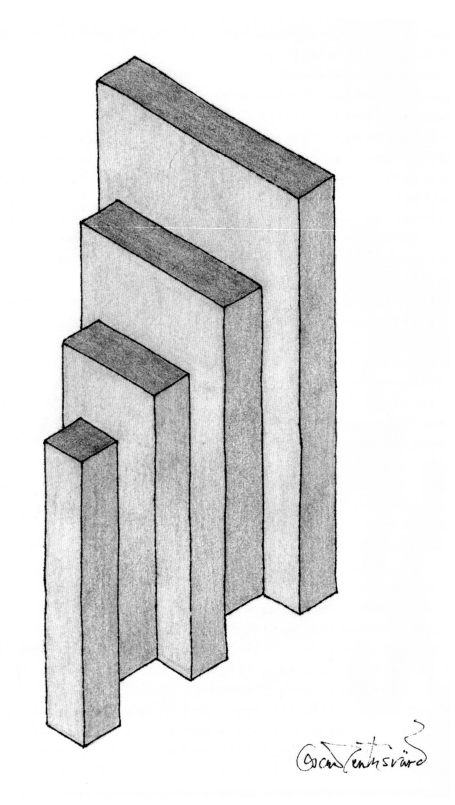

"Twisted Sides," colored felt-tip pen drawing, Japanese rice paper, undated,
12 × 9 inches (30.5 × 23 cm)

"Variations on an Impossible Triangle," colored felt-tip pen drawing, Japanese Rice paper,
undated, 12 × 9 inches (30.5 × 23 cm)

There are many paradoxes contained within this figure.

"Folding Upon Itself," colored felt-tip pen drawing, Japanese rice paper, undated,
12 × 9 inches (30.5 × 23 cm)

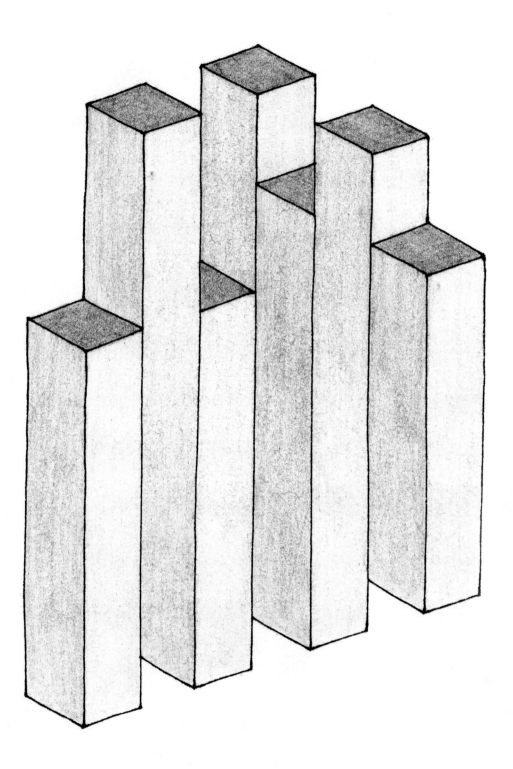

"Paradox 189," colored felt-tip pen drawing, Japanese rice paper, undated,
12 × 9 inches (30.5 × 23 cm)

"Paradox 135," colored felt-tip pen drawing, Japanese rice paper, undated,
12 × 9 inches (30.5 × 23 cm)

"Larger Pieces Fitting Within Smaller Pieces," colored India ink, undated,
22 × 14 inches (56 × 35.6 cm)

"Impossible Meander, #191," colored felt-tip pen drawing, Japanese rice paper, 1994,
12 × 9 inches (30.5 × 23 cm)

"My devil's fork was slightly different, by the way, to the figure subsequently published by Schuster [in 1965]; mine was derived from impossible meanders."

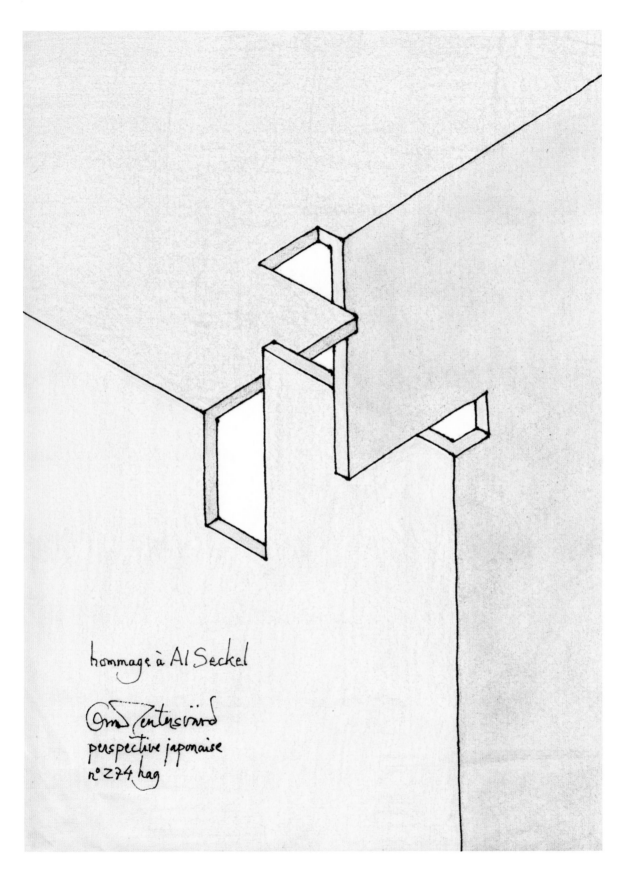

hommage à Al Seckel

[signature]
perspective japonaise
n° 274 hag

"IMPOSSIBLE CORNER, #274," COLORED FELT-TIP PEN DRAWING, JAPANESE RICE PAPER, 1994,
12 × 9 INCHES (30.5 × 23 CM)

109/120

"An Impossible Paradox in a Window," colored India ink, 22 × 14 inches (56 × 35.6 cm)

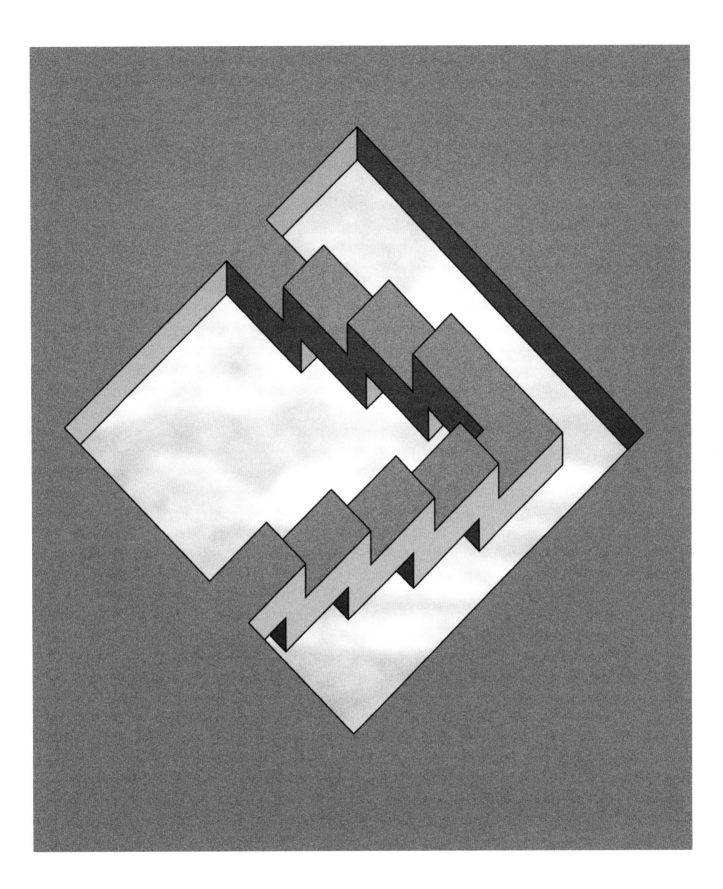

"Stairs Keeping their Own Level," colored India ink, undated, 22 × 14 inches (56 × 35.6 cm)

perspective japonaise n° 456 ac   Oscar Reutersvärd

"Paradox 456," colored India ink, undated, 22 × 14 inches (56 × 35.6 cm)

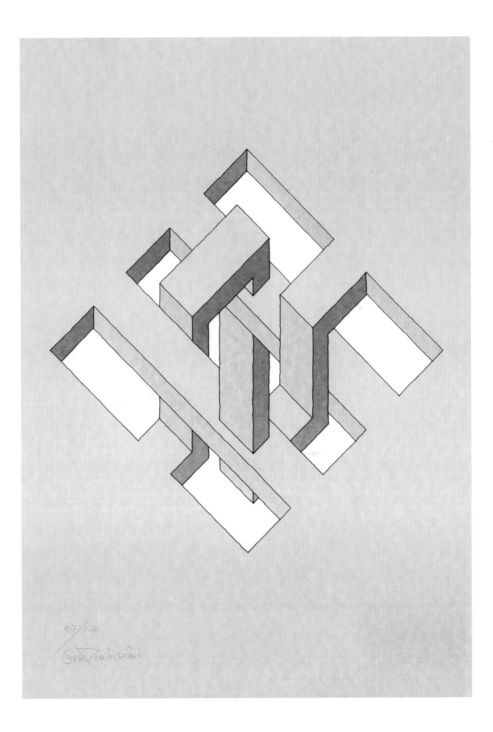

"MEANDER IN WINDOW," COLORED INDIA INK, UNDATED, 22 × 14 INCHES (56 × 35.6 CM)

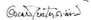

"PARADOX 6," COLORED FELT-TIP PEN
DRAWING, JAPANESE RICE PAPER, UNDATED,
12 × 9 INCHES (30.5 × 23 CM)

"PARADOX 161," COLORED FELT-TIP PEN
DRAWING, JAPANESE RICE PAPER, UNDATED,
12 × 9 INCHES (30.5 × 23 CM)

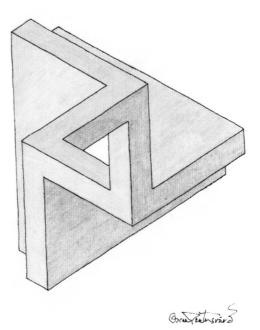

"PARADOX 29," COLORED FELT-TIP PEN
DRAWING, JAPANESE RICE PAPER, UNDATED,
12 × 9 INCHES (30.5 × 23 CM)

"PARADOX 219," COLORED FELT-TIP PEN
DRAWING, JAPANESE RICE PAPER, UNDATED,
12 × 9 INCHES (30.5 × 23 CM)

Reutersvärd filled many of his notebooks with impossible figures like these, where each impossible variation always suggested a new impossible figure to him.

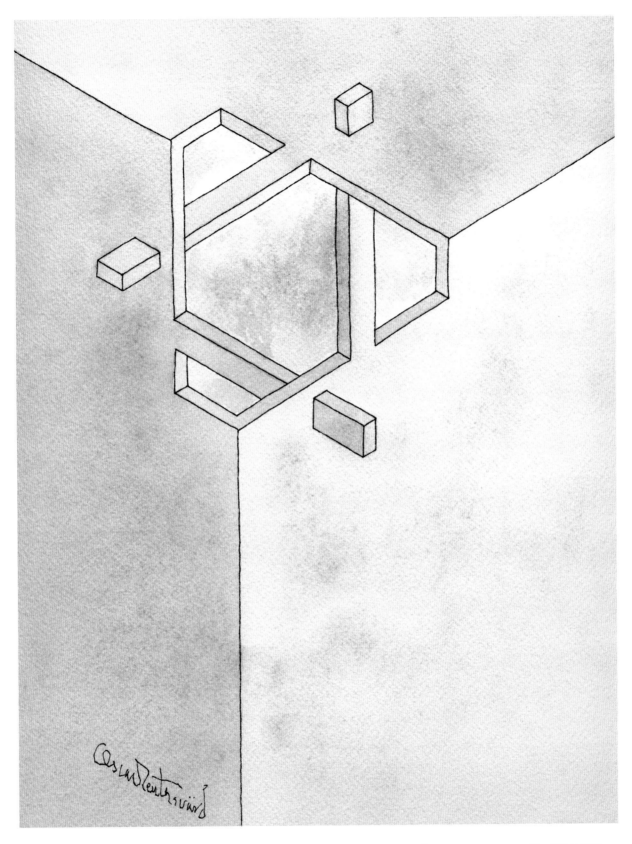

"CORNERING AN IMPOSSIBILITY," COLORED FELT-TIP PEN DRAWING, JAPANESE RICE PAPER, UNDATED,

12 × 9 INCHES (30.5 × 23 CM)

The more you examine this corner, the stranger it becomes.

CHAPTER 18

Roger Shepard

(1929–)

MIND SIGHTS

*"Psychologists know Roger Shepard as one of the most imaginative of their kind. . . .
How delightful to discover that he is an equally inventive artist: his drawings are as
witty and as thought-provoking as those of Escher himself."*

—PHILIP JOHNSON-LAIRD

Roger Shepard has always been a prankster. As a young boy, he delighted in playing visual tricks; one time he surreptitiously moved all the furniture out of his sister's room. Shepard went on to have an extremely distinguished career that included appointments at Harvard, Stanford, and U.C. Berkeley, all the while continuing to play visual tricks on people. By recording and analyzing their reactions, he would always discover new and astonishing truths about mental processes and human nature in general.

Roger Shepard was born in Palo Alto, California, in 1929. His father, a professor in materials science at Stanford, greatly encouraged and stimulated his son's interest in science and observing the environment. Shepard attended Stanford University, received his bachelor's degree in 1951, and earned his doctoral degree in experimental psychology from Yale in 1955. After a year of post-doctoral research at the Naval Research Laboratory and two years as a research associate at Harvard University, he became a member of the technical staff at Bell Labs, where he stayed until 1966. From there Shepard joined the faculty at Harvard as a full professor. Two years later he moved back to the Stanford campus where he remained for the next thirty years. After retiring from Stanford, he was appointed to the Hitchcock Professorship at U.C. Berkeley. In 1995, Shepard was awarded the nation's highest scientific honor: the National Medal of Science for his pioneering work in cognitive and evolutionary psychology.

Shepard is best known for developing a computer-based method of identifying hidden patterns in data, and for synthesizing an auditory illusion of endlessly rising pitch. His particular research field lies in the "mental rotation" of objects. In addition to his scientific pursuits, Shepard takes an interest in art, music, and illusions. In 1990 he published the classic work *Mind Sights: Original Visual Illusions, Ambiguities, and Other Anomalies*, which contained many of his delightful pen-and-ink drawings. He wrote,

> The drawings . . . achieve their effects by means of various visual tricks. But to call them tricks is not to imply that they are without psychological significance. The tricks work by taking advantage of fundamental perceptual principles that have been shaped by natural selection in a three-dimensional world. Our ability to make pictures, which emerged only recently on an evolutionary time scale, enables us to present the eyes with visual patterns that systematically depart from the patterns that we and our ancestors experienced in nature. In considering the ways pictures can trick the eye, we can gain insight into the nature and ultimate source of the principles of visual perception.

Shepard's work has been a tremendous inspiration to many optical illusion artists, including, among others, Sandro Del Prete, Shigeo Fukuda, and István Orosz.

Shepard has since retired from teaching at Stanford and lives in Texas.

ROGER SHEPARD, 1979

Can you find what is impossible about this engine? Note that the water tank is in the shape of a Klein bottle, which is a surface that has neither an inside nor an outside.

"Beckoning Balusters," pen and ink, 1984

Can you see the figures (a play on the word "figure" in figure and ground) in between the columns? A life-sized row of three-dimensional columns of a similar design was constructed by David Barker for display in San Francisco's Exploratorium.

"Egyptian-Eyezed Tête-à-Tête," pen and ink, 1974

Which do you see: two heads in profile on either side of the candlestick, or one head behind the candlestick? This is a clever adaptation of the famous Dutch Gestalt psychologist Edgar Rubin's figure/ground illusion of two profiles on either side of a vase.

"Glee Turns Glum," pen and ink, 1974

Notice that Glee remains at the top and Glum on the bottom even when the whole picture is turned upside down.

"L'EGS-ISTENTIAL QUANDARY," PEN AND INK, 1974

Shepard created an interesting variation on the impossible fork in his depiction of an impossible elephant. To avoid the counting paradox with the number of legs, Shepard introduced the more conspicuous line discontinuity at the far right. Both these figures have discontinuous boundaries, but the impossible fork exhibits no unclosed lines.

"PERIODIC STABLE OF THE ELEPHANTS," PEN AND INK, 1974

A stable of impossible elephants as depicted from front to back.

"SARA NADER," PEN AND INK, 1974

According to Shepard, "'Sara' Nader exemplifies a somewhat different type of figure/ground ambiguity in which the two alternative figures are not strictly complementary. While the black area constitutes the figure in the other interpretation (with the black areas then corresponding to dark or shadowed portions of the figure)."

"THE 5IVE 5ENSES," PEN AND INK, 1974

About "THE 5IVE 5ENSES" Shepard writes, "Here, I set myself the challenge of integrating into one picture, for each of the five senses, (a) the verb appropriate to that sense (for example, see, for the sense of vision); (b) the noun for the organ of that sense (for example, eye); and (c) a graphic portrayal of that organ itself (for example, a picture of an eye). I gave myself license to depart from this constraint only for the fifth sense. For that, I incorporated the verb touch, but instead of a noun for the organ of touch, I included the expletive that may follow too sharp a touch: 'Ouch!' Also, in rendering the 'O' of Ouch!, I portrayed the organ for emitting that expletive. The organ of the sense of touch is represented by the sharply 'touched' finger—both in side view (as the top of the T) and in end view (as the dot of the exclamation point)."

Can you also find the hidden word "tongue" in the word "taste"?

"TERROR SUBTERRA," PEN AND INK, 1974

The two figures are identical in size, although the one in the background appears to be larger than the one in the foreground. This drawing is based on the classic Hallway perspective illusion.

CHAPTER 19

Dick Termes

(1941–)

SPHERICAL WORLDS

"The sphere allows me to express ideas which are above, below, and all around me."

—DICK TERMES

TERMESPHERES ARE SPHERICAL PAINTINGS that hang and rotate from ceiling motors. They provide the viewer with a most wonderful and unique illusory experience. While watching a Termesphere in motion, your perception will suddenly switch: one moment you are on the outside looking at a slowly turning painted sphere, and the next moment you are on the inside of the sphere looking out! The motion of the sphere even reverses. People explain this illusion in many different ways. Some feel like they are looking through the sphere to the back side. Some say the images in the rooms become dimensional and turn richer in color and are fluid or jelly looking. Termes thinks the illusion happens because we are more comfortable with having the room around us on the concave surface. While he puts the room on the outside or convex side of the sphere our minds work to push it back to the real, or the concave. Realistic subjects have been found to work better than abstract ones. This could be because abstract paintings might seem alright being on the sphere but real worlds should be around us. A nice thing about the Termes illusion is that it gets people personally involved with the painting.

The spheres are painted on the outside using a six-point perspective system in which the total up, down, and all-around environment is depicted on its surface. To help understand this concept, imagine you are inside a transparent ball. You copy everything you see outside the sphere onto the inside surface of the sphere and then move to the outside of the sphere to look in at what you were looking out at. This is the Termesphere. Termes says,

> I think of myself inside the sphere even though I am on the outside painting.
> When people see this illusion where the sphere seems concave they are seeing it
> as I imagine it.

This system of perspective attracts many mathematical and geometry thinkers to Termes' work. They are interested in how this system of perspective can allow the subjects to read correctly from any angle. They are interested that all lines drawn on the sphere are bisections of the sphere. They also like the idea that all parallel lines project to two vanishing points or poles and all cubical objects painted in these paintings project to all six points. The strong perspective cues helps to create the illusion because it is always pulling you into that far away vanishing point. Many of his spheres give the viewer the feeling they are "floating" in the middle of the room. Termes has painted over three hundred Termespheres in the last thirty-three years.

Termes was born in 1941 in San Diego, California while his father was in the shipyards for the war effort. He received his Bachelors degree in art from Black Hills State College, his Masters degree in painting from the University of Wyoming and an MFA in design from Otis Art Institute of Los Angeles. Termes started painting when he was a junior in high school in 1959. In 1969, as a graduate student at the University of Wyoming, Termes researched the idea of expanding perspective beyond the traditional one and two point perspective of the Renaissance artists. All of this work was done as drawings until one of the drawings seemed to bulge off the page. A fellow student suggested that this looked like a sphere so Termes decided to find a ball and see what it would look like painted as a spherical painting. The cube Termes painted on this ball gave him the feeling that he was inside the cube rather than looking at a cube on the outside of the ball. This was the beginning of a life time of work.

Termes has explored environments on the sphere from real worlds, to surreal, to geometric. He has created transparent spheres where you can see through to the back side. One of his transparent spheres is of the inside of St. Peters Basilica in Rome. An illusion happens with this sphere. The dark patterns across the transparent sphere will hardly read until the ball is spun. As soon as the sphere rotates your eye goes directly to the back side of the ball and the front side disappears. Termes says,

> This is one more example of how our minds would rather see the world on the
> concave around us than on the outside of a convex sphere.

Because of his fascination with illusions and geometry, he became very interested in the work of American architect Buckminster Fuller and the Dutch artist M. C. Escher.

Bucky Fuller gave me great spherical geometry to look at and Escher showed me ways to use that geometry in my artform.

He has traveled extensively, creating a series of spherical paintings devoted to great architectural interiors found worldwide. Termes states,

> Architecture, especially the interiors of great architecture , seems to have been ignored in art history. I find these interiors wonderful and great subject matter for my six-point perspective paintings; wrapping these real, total interiors onto the surface of the sphere is one of the hardest things I do. There is no room for error, if you get something wrong on one side, it will come around to the back side and not fit.

The sphere allows Termes to express ideas that have not been talked about before. he reminds us that patterns or geometry that fit on the sphere are totally different from the pattern or geometry that fit on the flat surface. The sphere is a different dimension. By adding motion to the sphere, one more dimension is added to the spherical paintings.

The sphere is a way of life for Termes. He makes his home with his wife, Markie Scholz (a noted puppeteer) in four geodesic domes that they constructed in the Black Hills of South Dakota.

The sphere has influenced both my work and my life. I have always thought the sphere was the most perfect shape the universe had to offer. If you are looking to create a beautiful art piece, why not start with the most beautiful canvas, the sphere?"

Additional works by Termes can be seen at http://neuro.caltech.edu/~seckel/mod/.

TERMES LOVES HIS CREATIONS, 2002

"INSPIRATIONS FOR ESCHER," ACRYLIC ON POLYETHYLENE PLASTIC, 1998, 15³/₄-INCH-DIAMETER SPHERE (40 CM)

The Dutch graphic artist M. C. Escher came upon many of his ideas in his favorite town of Ravello, Italy. According to Termes, "Ideas are around us all the time, but only some people see them. Most of the ideas around him are not what the images look like when he transformed them into his famous art pieces." This environment is one of the small roadways within Ravello, Italy, which was such a great source of inspiration for Escher.

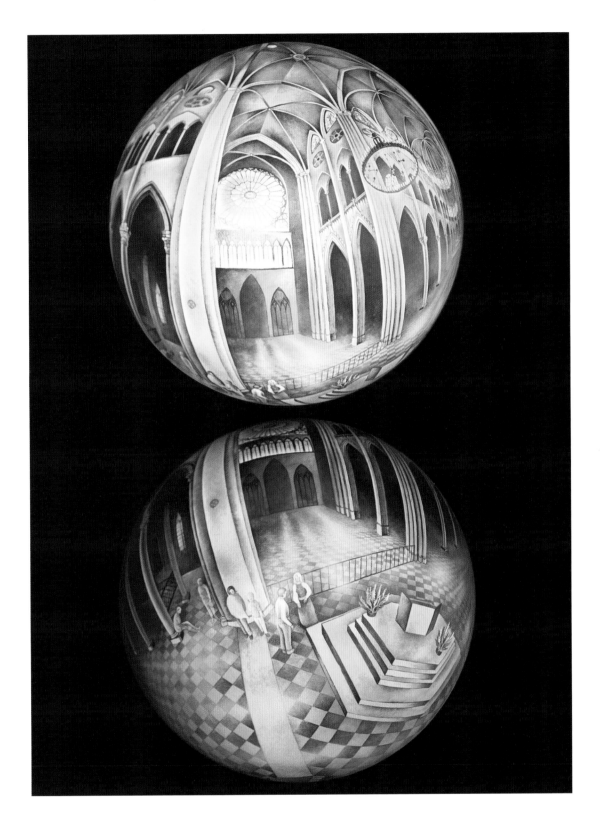

"NOTRE DAME," ACRYLIC ON POLYETHYLENE PLASTIC, 1995, 24-INCH-DIAMETER SPHERE (61 CM)

This spherical painting was developed during Termes's visit to the Notre Dame cathedral in Paris in 1992. When viewing this painted sphere, the observer will get the impression that he or she is floating and revolving thirty feet above the floor in the center of Notre Dame. Usually Termes uses six-point perspective to make his spherical paintings work, but in this case the floor's diagonal tiling required four more vanishing points, which, when added, allowed for a ten-point perspective.

"ESCHER TO THE THIRD POWER," ACRYLIC ON POLYETHYLENE PLASTIC, 1983,
16-INCH-DIAMETER SPHERE (40.5 CM)

This spherical painting plays off M.C. Escher's 1938 self-portrait "Hand with Reflective Sphere," which depicts the artist holding a spherical reflective ball in his hand with his surroundings also reflected in the mirror. Escher was fascinated by the fact that the point between your eyes is always in the absolute center of the mirrored ball. Termes took up this thought and showed how the total picture Escher sought can be equally spaced or pulled around the sphere. The picture on the right was the only part Termes had to make up as the rest could be found in Escher's print. Escher's real hand was also removed to leave only the reflection.

DETAILS OF "ESCHER TO THE THIRD POWER"

"LORETTO CHAPEL," ACRYLIC ON POLYETHYLENE PLASTIC, 1991, 24-INCH-DIAMETER SPHERE (61 CM)

The Loretto in the Round is a chapel in Santa Fe, New Mexico, which is famous for its spiral staircase. Termes spent seven days inside the chapel sketching the staircase's surroundings. The lines within this chapel are projected to six equidistant vanishing points. Each line, if extended, would target two different vanishing points and would create a great circle if fully extended.

"Paris Opera," acrylic on polyethylene plastic, 1992-1993, 15³/₄-inch-diameter sphere (40 cm)

If you were to put a mirrored ball on the post next to the staircase going into the Paris Opera house, and if you could freeze the image onto that ball, you would come close to this Termesphere. Termes also played off the musical *Phantom of the Opera*, which was based on this building. One of the masks of the Phantom is a double-image superimposed on the archway in the building. The bottom of the sphere shows the stairway circling and going back under itself.

"THE PANTHEON," ACRYLIC ON POLYETHYLENE PLASTIC, 1998, 12-INCH-DIAMETER SPHERE (30.5 CM)

If you were inside this sphere, it would make perfect sense. You would be standing in the middle of the Pantheon where the floor and the ceiling geometry reads pure. It was possible to paint because Termes had taken panoramic shots of the entire cathedral the year before. For Termes, the Pantheon was a perfect subject because it was designed as a sphere itself, placed atop a cylinder wall. Standing on the floor in the center of the Pantheon puts you conceptually on the edge of the sphere. This sphere was painted in 1998 for the Escher Centennial Congress.

"SAINT MARK'S SQUARE," ACRYLIC ON POLYETHYLENE PLASTIC, 2001, 24-INCH-DIAMETER SPHERE (61 CM)

Imagine you had a transparent sphere on your head and you copied the Saint Mark's Square environment around you on the inside of the sphere. Now if you take that spherical painting off your head and move to the outside to look at it, this painting is what you would see, except it isn't backwards.

CHAPTER 20

Rex Whistler

(1905–1944)

INVERSIONS

"Whistler's exquisite lightness of touch, delight in the odd world around him, and teasing sense of fun are all brought out by his paintings and drawings."

—C. WHITWELL

No one knows when inverted images were first created, but they started to become popular on coins during the Reformation. These early topsy-turvy images typically contained hidden political and theological statements. In the 19th century, they took on a more amusing motif and were very popular in advertisements and puzzle cards.

In 1948, the world was introduced to the delightful topsy-turvy drawings of an English artist Rex Whistler, who had brought his portraits to new heights in a children's book entitled *OHO!* To accompany the twenty-five different faces, the book also contained satirical and comic verses written by his brother Laurence, a respected glass engraver. The book had no front or back, or rather had two of each. Although almost all of the images are original to Whistler, he did modify some topsy-turvy images that been circulating on various popular puzzle cards of the late 19th century. Whistler found it easier to create male than female topsy-turvy portraits, because a head of hair could easily transform itself into a beard.

Whistler studied art at the Royal Academy School in London but was asked to leave after one term, apparently because his approach to art was considered too frivolous. His professor at the Slade School of Fine Art in London, where Whistler continued his studies, later wrote to the academy principal, thanking him for "sending me your best pupil!"

Whistler was also renowned for his *trompe l'oeil* decorations and fantastic storytelling murals. His mural "Pursuit of Rare Meats" in the Tate Gallery in London is a work of exceptional genius. He also designed furniture, buildings, theater sets, and costumes for national productions.

Whistler was a mature draughtsman at the age of twelve, and barely in his creative prime when he was killed at the age of thirty-nine: A mortar bomb exploded while he was trying to free a trapped tank on his first day of action in Normandy, France, in 1944. Before his untimely death, he had achieved some considerable fame for his illustrations of Jonathan Swift's *Gulliver's Travels* and Hans Christian Andersen's fairy tales.

"A King and His Queen," pencil drawing, undated, $6^{1}/_{2} \times 8^{1}/_{2}$ inches (16.5 × 21.5 cm)

The King is looking for his Queen. Can you find her?

"A Change of Expression," pencil drawing, undated, $6^{1}/_{2} \times 8^{1}/_{2}$ inches (16.5×21.5 cm)

A collar turns into a hat, and the mood changes.

"Surprise!", pencil drawing, undated, $6^{1}/_{2} \times 8^{1}/_{2}$ inches (16.5×21.5 cm)

The policeman looks surprised when you turn this drawing on its head.

"Growing Pains," pencil drawing, undated, $6^1/_2 \times 8^1/_2$ inches (16.5 × 21.5 cm)

A boy turns into a man when the drawing is rotated.

"Being Nosy on the Phone," pencil drawing, undated, $6^1/_2 \times 8^1/_2$ inches (16.5 × 21.5 cm)

"GROWING A BEARD," PENCIL DRAWING, UNDATED, $6^1/_2 \times 8^1/_2$ INCHES (16.5×21.5 CM)

When inverted, the man has grown a beard.

"CHANGING GAZE," PENCIL DRAWING, UNDATED, $6^1/_2 \times 8^1/_2$ INCHES (16.5×21.5 CM)

The direction of the gaze changes when the figure is inverted.

RECOMMENDED READING

Baltrusaitis, Jurgis. *Anamorphic Art*. New York: Harry Abrams, 1977.

——*Anamorphoses: Les Perspectives Dépravées*. Paris: Flammarion, 1984.

Block, J. Richard. *Seeing Double*. New York: Routledge Books, 2002.

Combs, Karen. *Optical Illusions for Quilters*. Shelton, CT: Image Graphics, 1997.

Dars, Célestine. *Images of Deception: The Art of Trompe- l'oeil*. Boston: Phaidon Press, 1979.

Dalí, Salvador, et al. Dawn Ades, ed. *Dalí's Optical Illusions*. New Haven, CT: Yale University Press, 2000.

Danto, Arthur. *The Art of John Cederquist: Reality of Illusion,* Exhibition at the Oakland Museum of California, Sept. 13–Nov. 30, 1997.

Del Prete, Sandro. *Illusoria.* Bern: Bentelli Verlag, 1987.

——*Illusorisme, Illusorismes. Illusorisms.* Bern: Bentelli Verlag, 1984.

de Meyere, J.A.L., and Hette Weijma, *Anamorfosen*. Amsterdam: Aramith Uitgevers, 1989.

d'Otrange Mastai, Marie-Louise. *Illusion in Art: Trompe L'Oeil: A History of Pictorial Illusionism*. New York: Abaris Books, 1976.

Emmer, Michele, and Doris Schattschneider (eds). *M. C. Escher's Legacy: A Centennial Celebration*. New York: Springer Verlag, 2003.

Emmer, Michele, ed. *The Visual Mind: Art and Mathematics*. Cambridge, MA: The MIT Press, 1993.

Ernst, Bruno. *The Eye Beguiled: Optical Illusions.* Cologne: Benedikt Taschen, 1986.

———*The Magic Mirror of M.C. Escher*. Norfolk: Tarquin Publications, 1985.

Escher, M. C. *Escher on Escher: Exploring the Infinite*. New York: Harry N. Abrams, 1989.

Fukuda, Shigeo. *Visual Illusion*, Rikuyoshi Publishing, 1982.

Füsslin, Georg, and Ewald Hentze. *Anamorphosen*. Stuttgart: Füsslin-Verlag, 1999.

Gombrich, E. H. *Art and Illusion: A Study in the Psychology of Pictorial Representation*. Boston: Phaidon Press, 1962.

Gonsalves, Rob. *Imagine a Night*. New York: Atheneum Books for Young Readers, 2003.

Gonsavles, Robert. *Imagine a Day*. New York: Atheneum Books for Young Readers, 2004.

Gregory, Richard, and E. H. Gombrich. *Illusion in Nature and Art*. New York: MacMillan, 1980.

Hofstadter, Douglas. *Gödel, Escher, Bach: an Eternal Golden Braid*. New York: Basic Books, 1979.

———*Metamagical Themas: Questing for the Essence of Mind and Pattern*. New York: Basic Books, 1985.

Hammond, Paul. *Upon the Pun: Dual Meaning in Words and Pictures*. London: W. H. Allen, 1978.

Hughes, Patrick. *Vicious Circles and Infinity: A Panoply of Paradoxes*. New York: Doubleday, 1975.

Kim, Scott. *Inversions: A Catalog of Calligraphic Cartwheels*. Emeryville, CA: Key Curriculum Press, 1996.

Kince, Eli. *Visual Puns in Design: The Pun Used As a Communications Tool*. New York: Watson-Guptill, 1982

Langdon, John. *Wordplay: Ambigrams and Reflections on the Art of Ambigrams*. Orlando, FL: Harcourt Brace Jovanovich, 1992.

Leeman, Fred, *Hidden Images: Games of Perception, Anamorphic Art, Illusion: From the Renaissance to the Present*. New York: Harry N. Abrams, 1975.

Livingstone, Margaret, *Vision and Art: The Biology of Seeing*. New York: Harry N. Abrams, 2002.

Locher, J. L. (ed.), *M.C. Escher; His Life and Complete Graphic Work*. New York: Abradale Press, 1992.

Néret, Gilles, and Robert Descharnes. *Salvador Dalí: The Paintings 1904–1989*. Cologne: Benedikt Taschen, 1993.

Parola, Rene. *Optical Art: Theory and Practice*. Weatogue, CT: Reinhold Books, 1969.

Penrose, Lionel, and Roger Penrose, "Impossible Objects: A Special Type of Visual Illusion," *British Journal of Psychology*, 1958, vol. 49, pp. 31-33.

Rothstein, Julian, and Mel Gooding. *The Playful Eye: An Album of Visual Delight*. San Francisco: Chronicle Books, 1999.

Schattschneider, Doris, and M. C Escher. *Visions of Symmetry: Notebooks, Periodic Drawings, and Related Work of M. C. Escher*. New York: W. H. Freeman, 1990.

Seckel, Al. *The Great Book of Optical Illusions*. Westport, CT: Firefly Books, 2002.

———*Incredible Visual Illusions: You Won't Believe Your Eyes*. Port St. Lucie, FL: Arcturus Books, 2003.

Shepard, Roger. *Mind Sights: Original Visual Illusions, Ambiguities, and Other Anomalies*. New York: W. H. Freeman, 1990.

Stafford, Barbara Maria and Frances Terpak, *Devices of Wonder: From the World in a Box to Images on a Screen*. Los Angeles: Getty Research Institute Publications, 2002.

Velhuysen, W. F. *The Magic of M. C. Escher*. New York: Harry N. Abrams, 2000.

Wade, Nicholas. *Visual Allusions: Pictures of Perception*. Mahwah, NJ: Lawrence Erlbaum Associates, 1990.

Zeki, Semir. *Inner Vision: An Exploration of Art and the Brain*. New York: Oxford University Press, 1999.

ARTIST INFORMATION & WEBSITES

Original signed prints, paintings, and sculptures may be obtained directly from the artists or their representatives. Please contact them via the information below.

SANDRO DEL-PRETE
Illusoria Land
Gewerbezone Ey 5
CH-3063, Ittigen, Switzerland
www.illusoria.com
e-mail: sandro@del-prete.ch

M.C. ESCHER
www.mcescher.com

SHIGEO FUKUDA
Fukuda Design Studio
3-34-25 Kamikitazawa, Setagaya-ku
Tokyo, Japan156

JOS DE MEY
Daalmstrasse 7
9930 Zomergem, Belgium

ROBERT GONSALVES
Discovery Galleries, Ltd.
4840 Bethesda Avenue
Bethesda, MD 20814
www.discoverygalleries.com

MATHIEU HAMAEKERS
Venlosesteen Weg 81
3640 Kinrooi/Ophoven
Belgium

SCOTT KIM
P.O. Box 2499
El Granada, CA 94018
www.scottkim.com
e-mail: info@scottkim.com

AKIYOSHI KITAOKA
www.ritsumei.ac.jp/~akitaoka/index-e.html
e-mail: akitaoka@Lt.ritsumei.ac.jp

KEN KNOWLTON
www.knowltonmosaics.com
e-mail: ken@knowltonmosaics.com

GUIDO MORETTI
www.guidomoretti.it/E_terzavia.htm
e-mail: modiug@libero.it

VIK MUNIZ
Brent Sikkema Gallery
530 W. 22nd Street
New York, NY 10011
www.vikmuniz.net
e-mail: gallery@brentsikkema.com

OCTAVIO OCAMPO
www.amazingartimages.com
e-mail: info@amazingartimages.com

ISTVÁN OROSZ
Reviczky U.20
H-2092 Budakeszi, Hungary
www.utisz.net
e-mail: utisz@axelero.hu

JOHN PUGH
John Pugh Studios
P.O. Box 1332
Los Gatos, CA 95031
www.artofjohnpugh.com

AL SECKEL
http://neuro.caltech.edu/~seckel
e-mail: seckel@klab.caltech.edu

DICK TERMES
Dick Termes Studios
1920 Christensen Drive
Spearfish, SD 57783
www.termespheres.com
e-mail: termes@blackhills.com

INDEX

CREDITS

5 Courtesy Douglas R. Hofstadter

9 William Hogarth, "Perspectical Absurdities," engraved frontispiece from J. Kirby's *Dr. Brook Taylor's Method of Perspective Made Easy in Both Theory and Practice*, Ipswich, 1754

10 Andrea Pozzo, "Allegory of the Missionary Work of the Jesuits," Sant Ignazio, Rome. Courtesy the Rector of S. Ignazio

12 (top) Hans Holbein, "The Ambassadors," National Gallery London, U.K.

12 (bottom) Johan Burucker, Cylinder anamorphosis with Horse and Rider, Nürenberg, Germany, ca. 1800. Courtesy Hessisches Landesmuseum, Darmstadt

13 (top) Anonymous, Metamorphosis Landscape, 1600, private collection, Milan, Italy

13 (bottom) Matthaus Merian, "Campus Anthropmorphos," engraving, from Athanasius Kircher, *Ars Magna Lucis et Umbrae* 2nd ed (Amsterdam: Apud Joannem Janssonium 1671), opp. p 807

14, 15 (all) Author's private collection

16 René Magritte, "The Human Condition 1," private collection, Paris, France. Artists Rights Society

17 Reginald Neal, "Square of Three," New Jersey State Museum Collection, NJ, USA

20 Giuseppe Arcimboldo, "Self-portrait," Narodra Gallery, Prague, Chechnia

21 Giuseppe Arcimboldo, "Spring," Musée du Louvre, Paris, France

22 Giuseppe Arcimboldo, "Summer," Kunsthistorisches Museum, Vienna

23 Giuseppe Arcimboldo, "Autumn," Musée du Louvre, Paris, France

24 Giuseppe Arcimboldo, "Winter," Musée du Louvre, Paris, France

25 Giuseppe Arcimboldo, "Earth," private collection

26 Giuseppe Arcimboldo, "Air," private collection, Basel, Switzerland

27 Giuseppe Arcimboldo, "Fire," Gemäldegaleri Kunsthistorisches Museum, Vienna, Austria

28 Giuseppe Arcimboldo, "Water," Gemäldegaleri Kunsthistorisches Museum, Vienna, Austria

29 Giuseppe Arcimboldo, "The Jurist," Statens Konstsamlingar Gripsholm Slott, Sweden

30 Giuseppe Arcimboldo, "The Librarian," Statens Konstsamlingar Gripsholm Slott, Sweden

31 Giuseppe Arcimboldo, "The Vegetable Gardner," Museo Civico Ala Ponzone, Cremona, Italy

32 Giuseppe Arcimboldo, "Vertumnus," Skoklosters Slott, Stockholm, Sweden

34 Dalí photo

35 Salvador Dalí, "Paranoiac Visage," whereabouts unknown, probably destroyed

36 Salvador Dalí, "The Great Paranoiac," Museum Boymans-van Beuningen, Rotterdam, Germany

37 Salvador Dalí, "Apparition of Face and Fruit Dish on a Beach," The Wadsworth Atheneum, CT, USA

38 Salvador Dalí, "Mysterious Mouth Appearing in the Back of my Nurse," private collection

39 Salvador Dalí, "Disappearing Bust of Voltaire," The Salvador Dalí Museum on loan from E. and A. Reynolds Morse

40 Salvador Dalí, "The Hallucinogenic Toreador," The Salvador Dalí Museum on loan from E. and A. Reynolds Morse

41 Salvador Dalí, "Three Glorius Enigmas of Gala" (second version), courtesy Fundación Gala- Dalí, Figueras, Spain

42, 43, 44 Author's private collection

45 Salvador Dalí, "Dali's hand Drawing Back the Golden Fleece in the Form of a Cloud to Show Gala the Dawn, Completely Nude, Very, Very far away Behind the Sun," courtesy Fundación Gala- Dalí, Figueras, Spain

46 Salvador Dalí, "Gala's Christ," private collection

49 Author's private collection

50–65 (all) Courtesy and copyright Sandro Del Prete

68 Author's private collection

69–80 (all) Courtesy and copyright Jos De Mey

83 courtesy Bruno Ernst

84–93 All M.C. Escher prints are reproduced with permission from the archives of the M.C. Escher Foundation/Cordon Art, Baarn, Holland

96 Courtesy Kazumi Kurigami

97–113 (all) Courtesy and copyright Shigeo Fukuda

117 courtesy Discovery Galleries

117–130 (all) Courtesy and copyright Robert Gonsalves

132 courtesy Bruno Ernst

133–135 (all) Courtesy and copyright Matheau Hamaekers

136 The IllusionWorks logo is a registered trademark of IllusionWorks, L.L.C.

139–146 (all) Courtesy and copyright Scott Kim

About the Author

Al Seckel is the leading authority on visual and other types of sensory illusions. He lectures extensively on this topic at many of the world's most prestigious universities. He is the author of several best-selling and award-winning books on the science of optical illusions and perception. He is the author of the monthly Neuroquest column in *Discover* magazine and Brain Teasers in *National Geographic KIDS*. In addition, he designs interactive galleries on illusions for science museums. He is researching the neural correllates of visual illusions at the California Institute of Technology in Pasadena. His home page is: http://neuro.caltech.edu/~seckel.